THE POWER OF SPOKEN AND UNSPOKEN WORDS

Pastor Gil Kaplan

The Power of Spoken and Unspoken Words

Copyright © 2015 Gil Kaplan

ISBN 13: 978-519878-253-3

ISBN 10: 1-51978-253-5

Cover Design by: Jason Sharp

Editing by: Beth Compton

Interior Design by: Jason Sharp

www.buildersofunity.com

ENDORSEMENTS

"Pastor Gil Kaplan is a truly gifted teacher and a man of the Word. We are told in Proverbs 18:21 that The Tongue has the power of life and death, and those who love it will eat its fruit. For good or bad, blessings or cursing, our words will shape our outcomes and impact the people around us.

Pastor Kaplan's book, The Power of Spoken and Unspoken Words has dug deep into this vital topic. The end result is a book of great substance and depth, whose pages can - and will change your life."

Messianic Rabbi Jonathan Bernis, President and CEO

Jewish Voice Ministries, International, Phoenix, Arizona

Author of: *A Rabbi Looks at Jesus of Nazareth, A Rabbi Looks at the Last Days, A Rabbi Looks at the Afterlife*

"The Power of Spoken and Unspoken Words by

Rabbi Gil Kaplan is truly a deep-cutting sword of the Holy Spirit. I rarely say this about any work, but I truly believe that anyone who's interested in walking closer with God will be greatly benefited, helped, affected and blessed by reading this wonderful, anointed book. I am confident that everybody who reads this book will have his heart touched by the Father."

Messianic Rabbi K A Schneider

Discovering The Jewish Jesus, Blissfield, Missouri

<u>Author of:</u> *Self-Deliverance*

———◆———

"I endorse this book because of my own personal experience which testify to the truth contained within these pages. This is a timely word, because it is written in an era when many speakers are focusing on the subject of using our words carefully and recognizing their power.

This book is like the second half of the rainbow; we have seen one side or the other, but seldom both sides at once. For years, I have watched Gil and his wife Brenda live the expression of love, always ready with a smile or a word for all.

Brilliantly utilizing his line by line approach throughout this teaching, Pastor/Rabbi Gil Kaplan leaves the reader no excuse to be powerless nor careless as he explains the subject and supports his position by the pillars of truth in God's Word."

Iverna M. Tompkins, D. D.

Iverna Tompkins Ministries International, Scottsdale, Arizona

Author of: *God and I, The Way to Happiness*

"We don't always realize how important it is to wisely choose our words, nor do we understand the power those words hold. We often forget that God created all things by His word! Rabbi Gil Kaplan's book, The Power of Spoken and Unspoken Words is a must for every serious follower of God's purpose in their lives.

Rabbi Gil's wise council and teachings have frequently blessed many congregants here at Arrowhead Messianic Congregation over the years. I have known Rabbi Gil and his wife Brenda for over 13 years and they have influenced my life greatly with their incredible support, wisdom, and kindness.

His profound instruction and thoughtful scriptural analysis of any subject is strong and lasting, whether it is about brokenness or the power of words. When Rabbi Gil teaches, it's time to get out the knife and fork, for there is no fluff to be had; only meat and potatoes which are what the body of Messiah needs today. He will cause you to search your heart to expose any hindrance to a proper relationship with our Lord and Savior Yeshua."

Messianic Rabbi Allan Moorhead

Arrowhead Messianic Congregation, Peoria, Arizona

"At the risk of sounding overly-dramatic, I truly believe the answer to the question, "What is the meaning of life?" is found in this book. Rabbi Kaplan has masterfully pinpointed the human condition, and how the usage of words (as well as the lack thereof) affects every individual, for better or for worse. Backed up most importantly by Scriptural truths throughout, Rabbi Kaplan touches on how words build up or tear down and how encouragement is one of the most powerful tools we have.

There are no words (pun intended) that can adequately describe the need for a book like this, at a time like this in our history and generation. I heartily and enthusiastically endorse this book, and am confident it will be one of the most important works you've ever had the blessing of reading through"

Messianic Rabbi Jack Zimmerman

Staff Evangelist, Jewish Voice Ministries International

Congregational Leader, Tree of Life Messianic Congregation Phoenix, Arizona

———⟡———

"This teaching about the power of words especially hit home for me. I grew up in a large family, in a broken home, where there was a lot of violence. No loving words were spoken – only critical, hateful words, spoken out of a mean spirit, meant to humiliate and make others cry. No encouragement, no "thank you's," no appreciation of any kind. I was eleven years old before I realized that "Jesus Christ" was not a swear word. My late brother's salvation in 1972 set me on the path to the Savior.

I went into law enforcement, first in the prison system, then as a 911 operator. It was pounded into my head during training that the most powerful weapon I had was my mouth – they said that the words I used with people could either escalate or de-escalate a difficult situation. The same principle is taught in scripture and applies both at work and at home. Your words can bring peace, joy and harmony – or hatred, misery and *pain. Rabbi Gil brilliantly uses scripture and anecdotes to teach you to use your gift of speech the way that God intended us to use it – to uplift, encourage, exalt, hearten and love one another, "as He has loved us." He demonstrates how dangerous unkind words are, the permanent damage that can be caused – but he also shows us how powerful it can be for someone to be able to hear a positive word of encouragement, a "thank you" to acknowledge a service they've done in your behalf, or a sincere apology when they've been hurt. There is an old saying that "talk is cheap," but that's not true. Words are free, but their impact can last forever."*

Beth Compton

Friend and Managing Editor at EGGcellent Editing, Glendale, Arizona

ACKNOWLEDGEMENTS

This book is the fulfillment of all the encouragement, prophetic words and powerfully anointed prayers from family and friends that have been spoken and prayed over my teaching ministry. Their words were like "this should be a book" or "when is your book going to be published". And soon the Lord began bringing people that could help me.....so I must acknowledge my deepest gratitude to some of the great support from the following people without whom this book would not have been possible:

First and foremost I want to thank my precious and beloved wife Brenda, my best friend and powerful intercessor for "being there" to encourage, support and pray for me. She's worked tirelessly typing, researching and helping to edit this manuscript. Her Godly wisdom, input and insight has been such a blessing to help birth this book.

A very special word of gratitude goes to my wonderful Managing Editor and friend Beth Compton who has a lot of experience in editing teachings, manuscripts, articles, etc. She has an eye to catch the smallest punctuation or error and the mind to put every statement in its rightful and most impactful place. She truly is a gifted and anointed vessel of the Lord and her experience has been invaluable.

Next I want to thank the man whom the Lord used to jumpstart this project, Jason Sharp. One day he asked if he could help me publish my book after he and his wife listened to my two CD's on this subject. And just that simple statement started the ball rolling for this book. He's been such a blessing and very gifted and knowledgeable in guiding me through this process of formatting, cover design as well as getting everything setup for publication. I owe him a debt of gratitude for hearing from God and reaching out to me.

My sincerest thanks to Marti Sharp, Jason's wife for aggressively promoting the circulation and sales of the audio CD version of this teaching before and after its publication.

I am also deeply indebted and thankful to numerous authors that I have gathered thoughts and ideas from their books, emails, magazines and articles on the importance of our words and being a better listener.

It's with my deepest gratitude and such an honor to have my pastor, Dr. Michael Maiden to write the Foreword and to all my dear ministry friends who graciously wrote an Endorsement for this book.

Finally, and most importantly, I am so thankful for my Savior Jesus Christ who through the Holy Spirit gave me the grace and inspiration for this teaching in His perfect timing.

TABLE OF CONTENTS

FOREWORD

Rabbi Gil Kaplan has written a wonderful book that will help any believer become strong and successful in their journey with Christ. Our words matter "death and life are in the power of the tongue" and as followers of Jesus, the Holy Spirit wants to take over the "steering wheel" of our lives, our words. As you read this powerful book you'll discover many beautiful scriptures and anointed teaching about the power of your words. Rabbi Kaplan teaches us about how to bring a transformation into our mouth and words by experiencing a heavenly change in our heart. This book will also help you to become motivated to build up, heal and help your brothers and sisters in the body of Christ by the things you say. I've had the real privilege of knowing Rabbi Gil for many years and have witnessed the wisdom and love that he consistently expresses to others by the things he says. This book contains an important message that the messenger has lived. Read and be blessed!

Dr. Michael Maiden

Senior Pastor, Church for the Nations, Phoenix, Arizona

Author of: *Turn the World Upside Down, Joshua Generation, Elements. 8 Simple Rules, The Ancient Doors, Targeting the Ecclesia*

PREFACE

We all need help understanding the value of talking less and learning to be better listeners. Maybe you've heard these words, or perhaps spoken them yourself:

"You never stop talking!"

"You always keep interrupting!"

"You never listen!"

Words contain a lot of power and it's important that you learn to choose them carefully. How you say something is as important as what you say – maybe even more important.

Understanding the power of your words and when to use them effectively is vital to minimize regrets and maximize results. Also, just because you can say something doesn't necessarily mean that you should. Understanding the subtle difference between words that help and words that harm can be overshadowed by emotions such as anger, hurt, bitterness and unforgiveness. Therefore, speaking out doesn't always mean it's beneficial. Perhaps most importantly, how you

3

choose to say things is just as important as choosing when to say them.

This can be a real challenge for those of us who tend to speak first, without thinking. I am sure that every one of us has thought, "Why did I just say that?"

The lessons in this book are taken from a practical and a biblical standpoint to use wisdom in knowing what to say, how to say it, and when to say nothing at all. We should all weigh our words and think before we speak. Less talking really can equal better listening, thus opening up the door for better communication. Not only with each other, but it's vital for our relationship with the Lord.

It's my sincere wish that the pages of this book will give you a deeper understanding and offer greater hope for those who struggle to control your tongues. I pray that you will allow this teaching to bring spiritual purpose into your life, as well as the wisdom in knowing when to speak up, and when to remain silent. Words matter. By them we give meaning to everything.

Pastor Gil Kaplan

CHAPTER 1

DEATH AND LIFE ARE IN THE POWER OF THE TONGUE...WORDS REALLY MATTER.

I've chosen two main scriptures for this teaching:

Proverbs 18:20, 21 declares, *"A man's stomach shall be satisfied from the fruit of his mouth; From the produce of his lips he shall be filled. Death and life are in the power of the tongue, And those who love it will eat its fruit."*

The Message Bible says it this way; "Words kill, words give life; they're either poison or fruit—you choose."

The preacher in Eccles. 3: 1 and 7 says, *"To everything there is a season, A time for every purpose under heaven, A time to tear, And a time to sew; A time to keep silence, And a time to speak."*

If there is any place in our life that we need to exercise discipline and self-control, it's in how we choose our words when communicating with others.

Nothing has more power to enrich life or to make life miserable than do relationships. Most Christians struggle with the challenge of building healthier relationships. We all want to know how to structure our words and actions to assure others that we are truly interested in them. (1)

The words we speak have more power for good or evil than most of us may realize. Just one spoken word can change everything for either good or bad. Words can create or destroy relationships. They can make our lives brighter or darker. They can hurt or they can heal. Our words are capable of striking fear or they can bring inexpressible joy.

Because of a misuse of the spoken word destinies have been derailed, disunity has replaced unity and entire nations have been destroyed. Our very lives both physical and spiritual, depend upon our ability and willingness to speak out at the proper moment. (2)

There is no subject in the Bible that we should take any more seriously than the mouth. It can be used to bring blessing or destruction not only to our lives but also to the lives of many others.

Both silence and speaking up have two sides. One side can be positive and appropriate, the other side can be negative and inappropriate.

Silence. Speaking up. Both change destinies. When we use the tools inappropriately, we can do great harm. And when we use them as God intended, we can change our world for the better. (3)

Later in this teaching you will learn the answer on how we distinguish between these two sides of speaking up and silence.

It is my hope and prayer that you will allow this teaching to bring spiritual wisdom and purpose into your life about when to speak up and when not to.

Mistakes and missed opportunities are a part of our growth cycle in life. There will be times when we speak out in haste, instead of remaining silent and there will be times we are silent when a powerful, commanding voice should come forth. (4)

An example that comes to mind is the story of a mother who fell under conviction because of her habit of berating her nine-year old son. She would often lose her temper, saying things to him she knew were deeply hurtful to his self-esteem and to their relationship. One day in prayer, she made a vow to God that she would never again say anything demeaning to him. She had hardly finished her prayer when the front door opened and slammed shut with enough force to shake the whole house. Her son, Billy was home from school. The mother's anger swept over her as she thought, "How many times have I told him not to slam that door!"

Billy came into the den where she was, wordlessly threw his lunch pail on the floor and ran down the hallway to his bedroom. Before she could respond to his seeming defiance, he deliberately slammed the bedroom door.

Angrily, she said, "I'm going to get that kid. He knows better than that!" She rushed down the hallway, her temper raging, angry words ready to fly out of her mouth. As she put her hand on the bedroom door, the voice of God arrested her. "Didn't you just make a vow to me that you would never again verbally abuse your son?"

"Yes, Lord, but..."

"Then take your hand off that door, stand there for a moment and let me give you strength." She felt her anger receding and a calm flowing through her.

After a few minutes, she opened the bedroom door. Billy was lying across the bed, sobbing face down into the pillow. She sat down beside him and gently rubbed his back. Finally he looked up at her, wiping the tears from his cheeks. "What's the matter, son?" she gently asked.

"Mom, this has been the worst day of my life," Billy answered. "My best friend told me he doesn't like me anymore, and I flunked my math test." (5)

This book is not intended to create guilt or condemnation about those times we make errors in judgment. Instead, it is hoped that each one of us can evaluate our past choices and gain valuable insights into our own personal lives, thus influencing our future decisions with wisdom. On that day, a mother and her son learned a lesson of life that would forever enhance their relationship. *"The tongue has the power of life and death."* (Prov. 18:21)

Much of what we are experiencing today is the result of what we were speaking in the past. Of course, not everything in one's future is determined by his words; however, in real ways, our spoken words are seeds that bloom in future hopes and fears; they are trail blazers of our future, the pioneer of our tomorrows.

Still, most of us are too casual, or ignorant, about the weightiness of our words. It was Jesus Himself who warned in Mt 12:36, 37 *"For every idle word men may speak, they will give account of it in the day of judgment."* He continued, *"For by*

9

your words you will be justified, and by your words you will be condemned."

We will—each and every one of us—stand before God and give an account for our words and we will actually be justified or condemned by the things we uttered in life. How sobering—or how terrifying—this should be to every one of us.

CHAPTER 2

GOD CREATED THE WORLD WITH THE POWER OF HIS WORDS

Now, let's look closely at one of God's most incredible gifts to mankind and consider the potential we have right under our noses. . . words!

John 1:1 declares, *"In the beginning was the word, and the word was with God, and the word was God."*

To paraphrase Gen. 1:1-26, "At the beginning of time when God created the world and stocked the seas with marine life and the skies with winged creatures – when He caused the stars to ignite the night sky and placed the sun to light the day and the moon to illuminate the darkness." He did so with WORDS.

And God said, "Let there be light and God said,

let there be an expanse between the waters to separate water from water. And God said, let the water under the sky be gathered to one place, and let dry ground appear. And God said, let there be lights in the expanse of the sky to separate the day from the night

And God said, "Let the water teem with living creatures, and let birds fly above the earth across the expanse of the sky." And God said "let the land produce living creatures according to these kinds."

And God said, "Let us make man in our own image, in our likeness, and let them rule over the fish of the sea and the birds of the air, over the livestock, over all the earth, and over all the creatures that move along the ground" - and it was so.

God spoke and what was not became what is. It's amazing and wonderful to think that when God created the heavens and the earth, He used a mighty force. The power of His WORDS.

Heb. 11:13 says, *"By faith we understand that the worlds were framed by the word of God."*

Psa. 33:6 declares, *"By the word of the LORD the heavens were made, And all the host of them by the breath of His mouth."*

Equally amazing is that when God created mankind in His own image, He gave us that same powerful tool, WORDS. The power to use words is a very unique and powerful gift from God. Of all the creatures on this planet only man has the ability to communicate through the spoken word. Though it is a gift, it is still a double-edged sword because our words have the power to destroy and the power to build.

Think of your own lives, and this amazing gift that God has given to you. Are you using words to build up others or tear them down? Are your words filled with hate or love? Encouragement or discouragement? Bitterness or blessing? Complaining or compliments? Victory or defeat? Life or death?

Words do more than merely convey information. "Our words also have creative potential. They can create a smile on a discouraged child's face; lighten the heart of a husband loaded down with burdens; fan into a flame the dying embers of a friend's smoldering dreams; cheer brothers and sisters in Christ to run the race with endurance and bring the message of the hope and healing of Jesus Christ to a wounded world." (1)

As committed followers of Jesus, I believe we must routinely reflect on the kind of words we have chosen to speak. Like tools they can be used to help us reach our goals, or send us spiraling into a deep depression.

13

Words are the containers for power. God gave us this ability to love people through our encouraging, positive, life-giving words.

With our tongues we defend or destroy, heal or kill, cheer or criticize. Our words can make or break a marriage, paralyze or propel a friend, sew together or tear apart a relationship, build up or bury a dream, curse God or confess Jesus as Lord and Savior.

Just as God used words to create physical life our words can be the spark to generate spiritual life through the new birth or born again experience. Words are one of the most powerful forces in the universe and astoundingly, God has entrusted them to you and me. What an awesome responsibility!

Paul declared in Romans 10:9, 10, *"That if you confess with your mouth the Lord Jesus and believe in your heart that God has raised Him from the dead, you will be saved. For with the heart one believes unto righteousness, and with the mouth confession is made unto salvation."*

Amazingly, it is with our mouths, or words that we are saved and that is a radical responsibility. That realization is potently powerful.

This issue about words is very personal to God. It concerns how we talk about ourselves, our spouses, our children, our churches, our cities and nations.

Our words should be aligned with the words of Jesus, who only did and said what He saw His Father doing and saying and this should always be our example to follow.

Wouldn't it be glorious if we modeled why, when, and how Jesus spoke or remained silent? I believe it would certainly eliminate a lot of the problems we face. In these perilous times we live in, it is imperative upon us to know His words more than ever before, to align our words with His word. This is not only His written word, the Holy Scriptures, but the timely words that He speaks day-by-day and wants to release through us by becoming His mouthpiece.

CHAPTER 3

WORDS...WORDS...WORDS...AND MORE WORDS!

We sure use a lot of words don't we?!

Words really matter. By them we give meaning to everything.

Every day we speak countless words, often paying very little attention to the words themselves. It's estimated that the average person says about thirty thousand words every day. So in a lifetime, you or I could fill the Library of Congress with the words we have spoken. If we are not speaking words, we are typing words, texting words, tweeting words, or merely thinking words. Words determine which dreams live or die. Think about this, the words you speak and how you say them after a particular situation is over, whether life-giving or death, have the potential to impact people around you for hours, days, months, years and even a life-time.

Some seem to think our words simply fall to the ground and die or vanish into thin air and dissolve into nothingness. Not so! Our words live on, they do not die!

Emily Dickenson the famous American poet once said "A word is dead when it is said, some say. I say it just begins to live that day." (1)

There's a popular saying that says "everything on the internet lives forever." (2)

So to avoid painful regrets for having spoken negative words to someone, may your mouth always be filled with life-giving words.

We must watch and listen before we speak because there is truly life and death, good and evil in the tongue and God wants to add a new authority upon our words as His sons and daughters to speak life giving words into nations, people, and in all situations.

Have you ever considered that every word you choose once spoken has the power to either hurt or heal and can never be taken back? There is much wisdom in an old proverb worth remembering that says: Four things come not back: the sped arrow, time past, the neglected opportunity and the spoken word. In other words, don't use your time and words carelessly.

Neither can be retrieved or recalled.

Here is a story that will speak loud and clear about the tremendous impact of the words we speak. There was a parishioner in a small church that became disgruntled with some things one of the pastors had done. Maybe she was justified or at least had a right to her opinion.

Her first mistake, though, was to try to make her opinion everyone else's opinion. The more she talked about it, the angrier she became, and she began to embellish on the truth until the facts became nothing but lies. After a time of spreading these vicious rumors and lies about her pastor, she became convicted by the Holy Spirit and went to him, asking forgiveness.

The pastor took her to the top of the church where the steeple was and as they looked out over the little town from where they were standing he took a feather pillow and began shaking it over the edge until no more feathers were left in the pillow but were scattered from one end of the town to the other. The wind carried some way up in the sky, others floated to the ground. Some were getting stuck on tree branches and ledges of the building and some were being carried off by the wind until they were out of sight. Then the pastor said, "I choose to forgive you and I love you. But I want you to see something. Look how all these feathers have scattered, being carried off by the wind, some getting caught in objects, some we can't reach, some are temporarily hidden and the ones that are laying still will move again, once the wind begins to blow. That's how your words have become. We can never get all the feathers back to make this pillow look like it did before nor can we get back the damage from the impact of the words that were spoken."

Almost every word we say with our tongue impacts and shapes our thinking and the thinking of those who hear us. Those who hear us most are the most affected by our words. So we must always strive to edify, build up, comfort and encourage with Holy Spirit inspired sensitivity and wisdom. All of us are guilty at times of saying words to others without careful thought of the hurtful consequences. How wonderful it would be if we could learn to communicate in ways that we don't want to reverse or recall.

CHAPTER 4

RIGHT THINKING CAUSES RIGHT ACTIONS AND RIGHT WORDS!

There's a dynamic principle shown throughout the word of God and no person will walk in overcoming victory unless he or she understands and operates in it. And this dynamic principle is "Right thinking causes right actions and right words!"

There's a powerful connection that exists between our thoughts and our words and the two are linked together. Simply put, our thoughts become our words. And our words become our actions. Our words are a direct result of our thoughts and how we think is directly related to how we speak. What we meditate on is also directly related to how we think and speak. Your mouth gives expression to what you think, feel and want.

Language is the expression of thoughts; every time you speak, your mind is on parade, for all the world to see. It is an absolute necessity that our thinking, meditation and especially our speech line up with what God's word says about us as well as others.

An old Chinese proverb says "Be careful of your thoughts, they may become your words at any moment." (1) And author J.K. Rowling said, "Thoughts could leave deeper scars than almost anything else." (2)

It is very important to be accountable for our thoughts, because the root source of our words comes from our thoughts.

Since the problem with our words starts with thoughts, the remedy must begin there also and the Apostle Paul deals with this issue in the following three scriptures:

Paul encourages the Corinthians in II Cor. 10:3-5, *"For though we walk in the flesh, we do not war according to the flesh. For the weapons of our warfare are not carnal but mighty in God for pulling down strongholds, casting down arguments and every high thing that exalts itself against the knowledge of God, bringing every thought into captivity to the obedience of Christ."*

Paul admonishes us in Romans 12:1, 2, *"I beseech you therefore, brethren, by the mercies of*

God, that you present your bodies a living sacrifice, holy, acceptable to God, which is your reasonable service. And do not be conformed to this world, but be transformed by the renewing of your mind, that you may prove what is that good and acceptable and perfect will of God."

The inescapable truth is that the mouth will never be controlled unless the mind is controlled.

The Holy Spirit wants to control our mind but He never forces Himself on us. It is our choice. He leads us in the right direction by convicting us when we are thinking wrong thoughts.

We then have to choose to cast down the wrong thought and think on something that will bear good fruit....as we are instructed to do by Paul in Phil. 4:8, 9, *"Finally brethren, whatever things are true, whatever things are noble, whatever things are just, whatever things are pure, whatever things are lovely, whatever things are of good report, if there is any virtue and if there is anything praiseworthy—meditate on these things. The things which you learned and received and heard and saw in me, these do, and the God of peace will be with you."*

In Psa. 19:14 the Psalmist David prays, *"Let the words of my mouth and the meditation of my heart be acceptable in Your sight, O Lord, my strength and my Redeemer."*

23

Now please notice that he mentions both the mind and the mouth because they work together. Some people try to control their mouth, but they do nothing about their thoughts. That's like pulling the top off of a weed and how many know that unfortunately unless the root is dug up, the weed always comes back. As Christians all of us must purposely choose right thinking and right speaking. Britain's former Prime Minister Margaret Thatcher once quoted an old Chinese proverb, "Watch your thoughts they become words. Watch your words they become actions. Watch your actions they become habits. Watch your habits they become character. Watch your character it becomes your destiny. What we think we become."

Now the Bible tells us that God is omniscient. Omniscience is defined as "the state of having total knowledge, a quality of knowing everything."

For God to be sovereign over His creation of all things, whether visible or invisible, He has to be all-knowing. Therefore because of this reality God knows our every thought and every word on our tongue.

The Psalmist David declares in Psa. 139:1-4, *"O LORD, You have searched me and known me. You know my sitting down and my rising up; You understand my thought afar off. You comprehend my path and my lying down, And are acquainted with all my ways. For there is not a word on my tongue, But behold, O LORD, You know it altogether."* God not only knows what we said yesterday and what we are saying today, but also what we are going to say tomorrow and even what we are thinking.

And the final scripture on our thoughts is found in I Cor. 2:16 from the Amplified Bible states, *"For who has known or understood the mind (the counsels and purposes) of the Lord so as to guide and instruct Him and give Him knowledge? But you and I have the mind of Christ (the Messiah) and do hold the thoughts (feelings and purposes) of His heart."*

CHAPTER 5

OUT OF THE ABUNDANCE OF THE HEART THE MOUTH SPEAKS!

While it is the Holy Spirit that gives us power to change the words we speak, the desire to change begins in the heart. To state it another way, spiritual transformation begins in the mind and then filters down to the heart.

Philippians 4:6-7 reads: *"Be anxious for nothing, but in everything by prayer and supplication, with thanksgiving, let your requests be made known to God; and the peace of God, which surpasses all understanding, will guard your hearts and minds through Christ Jesus."*

The Bible has much to say about how the condition of our hearts affect our speech. The heart of the matter is a matter of the heart. The word "heart" in the New King James Version of the Bible is found 835 times in 775 verses.

Jer. 17:9, 10 declares, *"The heart is deceitful above all things, And desperately wicked; Who can know it? I, the LORD, search the heart, I test the mind, Even to give every man according to his ways, According to the fruit of his doings."*

Jer. 11:20 says, *"But, O LORD of hosts, You who judge righteously, Testing the mind and the heart, Let me see Your vengeance on them, For to You I have revealed my cause."*

In I Kings 8:39, speaking of God Solomon declares, *"For You alone know the hearts of all the sons of men."*

I Sam. 16:7 says, *"But the LORD said to Samuel, "Do not look at his appearance or at his physical stature, because I have refused him. For the LORD does not see as man sees; for man looks at the outward appearance, but the LORD looks at the heart."*

God can see things about you that no one else can see. Deep things. Hidden things. Those inner thoughts and desires that your family and friends have no idea are even floating around in your heart and mind. Don't fool yourselves; God knows all about them.

Heb. 4:12, 13 declares, *"For the word of God is living and powerful, and sharper than any two-edged sword, piercing even to the division of soul and spirit, and of joints and marrow, and is a discerner of the thoughts and intents of the heart. And there is no creature hidden from His sight, but all things are naked and open to the eyes of Him to whom we must give account."* Think about this. God's message is alive and active, penetrating the innermost part of a person. It distinguishes what is natural and what is spiritual, as well as the thoughts, reflection and intents of a person.

The word of God also exposes the natural and spiritual motivations of a believer's heart. The words "naked and open" in this scripture suggests complete exposure and defenselessness before God to whom all believers "must give account" to the all-seeing all-knowing God.

The word of God is the measuring stick Christ will use at the judgment seat according to II Cor. 5:10 that reads, *"For we must all appear before the judgment seat of Christ, that each one may receive the things done in the body, according to what he has done, whether good or bad."*

The quality of your words reveal the quality of your heart. The Lord Jesus said in Mt. 12:33-35 from the New Revised Standard Version, *"Either make the tree good, and its fruit good; or make the tree bad, and its fruit bad; for the tree is known by its fruit. You brood of vipers! How can you speak good things, when you are evil? For out of the abundance of the heart the mouth speaks. The good person brings good things out of a good treasure, and the evil person brings evil things out of an evil treasure."* Our words reveal what kind of heart we possess. Your words are actually windows to your heart. The words that escape our lips reveal the condition of our inner man. Your words are pictures of your heart and everything you say is a photograph of your heart.

Prov. 27:19 from the New Living Translation says, *"As a face is reflected in water, so the heart reflects the real person."*

The Message Bible Translation says it this way, *"just as water mirrors your face, so your face mirrors your heart."*

Actions reveal a believers spiritual maturity or lack of it but the heart reveals our deepest intentions.

Prov. 16:23 instructs, *"The heart of the wise teaches his mouth and adds learning to his lips."*

You can read the heart of any person by listening to the words they are speaking about others. Someone has said, "What is in the well of the heart will come out through the bucket of the mouth." (1) In other words - What's in our heart will eventually come out and sometimes our speech will betray us and that can become very embarrassing.

King Solomon, the wisest man who ever lived and who wrote the book of Proverbs under divine inspiration said in Prov. 23:7, *"For as he thinks in his heart, so is he."*

In Prov. 4:23 the New Living Translation says, *"Guard your heart above all else, for it determines the course of your life."*

Right thinking, right speaking and a pure heart are vitally important elements to living a victorious Christian life.

King David, Israel's greatest king knew about this principle and we see this throughout The Psalms. Pay close attention to David's words.

Psa. 24:3, 4 says, *"Who may ascend into the hill of the LORD? Or who may stand in His holy place? He who has clean hands and a pure heart, Who has not lifted up his soul to an idol, Nor sworn deceitfully."*

After his sins of murder and adultery, King David needed a new heart. But he knew that he was not capable of providing it for himself. So he asked God to do it as he prayed these touching words written in Psa. 51:10, 11, *"Create in me a clean heart, O God, And renew a steadfast spirit within me. Do not cast me away from Your presence, And do not take Your Holy Spirit from me."*

The word "create" is hugely significant because it reveals the fact that David knew he was powerless to fix his own heart.....it was too

31

messed up. David was asking that his heart be renewed, restored, and transformed. And God is the only source of such renewal.

In Psa. 139:23, 24 David invites God to *"Search me, O God, and know my heart; Try me, and know my anxieties; And see if there is any wicked way in me, And lead me in the way everlasting."*

These are perhaps some of the most poignant words in the entire Bible. In these two verses is so much agony, yet so much wisdom. We see David asking God to search him, to look to the deepest part of what he is, in his own heart. Why would he ask this? And, why would any of us ask it? Because we cannot know our own hearts as well as God can. He indwells us and He knows every thought and every word we speak, He is aware of every feeling, and understands us better than we do.

If we ever needed anyone to reach down into the very depths of our hearts to find out what is unholy so that it can be removed. It is God.

David is asking God to prove, to test his loyalty because he is not like the wicked men spoken of earlier in the Psalm. David desired God and His holiness.

Psa. 141:3, 4 declares, *"Set a guard, O LORD, over my mouth; Keep watch over the door of my lips. Do not incline my heart to any evil thing, To practice wicked works with men who work iniquity; And do not let me eat of their delicacies."*

This is a prayer crying out for wisdom, for restraining evil language, and for knowing the correct words to speak. David wanted to avoid any act of impiety, irreverence, or even idolatry; he did not want to offend God with anything he said. Anything that offends God in our conversation needs to be eliminated.

David says to the Lord in Psa. 17:3, *"You have tested my heart; You have visited me in the night; You have tried me and have found nothing; I have purposed that my mouth shall not transgress."*

As believers we have to do the right thing in this area. Whatever we do in this life of faith, we must do it on purpose. It is not necessarily easy, but it begins with a quality decision. Discipline is a choice. When we are frustrated with some sort of difficult situation, we will definitely have to purpose to keep our mouth from transgressing.

In the first part of Matthew chapter 15 Jesus was questioned by the scribes and Pharisees, basically saying why do your disciples transgress the traditions of the elders? For they do not ceremonially wash their hands when they eat bread to remove any defilement.

In Mt. 15:11 and verses 18-20 Jesus answers that question by saying *"not what goes into the mouth defiles a man, but what comes out of the mouth,...this defiles a man."*

In verses 18-20 of Mt. 15 Jesus continues, *"But those things which proceed out of the mouth come from the heart and they defile a man. For out of the heart proceed evil thoughts, murders, adulteries, fornications, thefts, false witness, blasphemies, these are the things which defile a man but to eat with unwashed hands does not defile a man."*

The Pharisees clung to outward religious rituals and the traditions of men but what God desired most was their hearts but they were hardened and cold. And Jesus continually pointed out the condition of the scribes and Pharisees' hearts.

We cannot act beyond what we believe, therefore, if we want to change the way we speak, then the first step is to check on the condition of our heart. We must follow the example of David, and ask God to examine us and to create a new heart within us.

How many of you want that for your lives?

CHAPTER 6

AS BELIEVERS WE HAVE A CHRISTIAN DUTY TO ENCOURAGE ONE ANOTHER

The greatest enemy you will ever face is **discouragement.**

We are all shaped by words from those who love us or refuse to love us. We are also shaped by words of those who don't even know our names. It is the heart's cry of all mankind to be loved and accepted and sometimes a simple word of encouragement can make all the difference. Never underestimate the power of a kind, encouraging word or deed. William Barclay said, "One of the highest of human duties is the duty of encouragement."

You should always choose your words with care and love. Cruel words deeply hurt; loving, kind and encouraging words quickly heal.

Prov. 12:25 from the Amplified Bible declares, *"Anxiety in a man's heart weighs it down, But a good (encouraging) word makes it glad."*

Prov. 16:24 from the New Living Translation teaches us that *"Kind words are like honey-sweet to the soul and healthy for the body."*

It's easy to laugh at men's ideals.

It's easy to pour cold water on their enthusiasm.

It's easy to discourage others.

The world is full of those willing to destroy and crush the hopes and dreams of others causing them to feel depressed, rejected, unloved, discouraged; and have low self-esteem. How many have found that out? A caring word can accomplish more than we could ever imagine. Our words become the mirror in which others see themselves. The human spirit rings with hope at the sound of an encouraging word. Little words and acts of kindness can bring a bit of heaven from above.

You can be a source of blessing and encouragement with your words every day. Many a time a word of praise, thanks, appreciation or cheer has kept a man from being discouraged and feeling like a failure. It has made a faint heart gain the courage necessary to carry on and accomplish what they were so willing to give up. Blessed is the man or woman who speaks such words of encouragement! Have you noticed that some people seem to have a way of brightening the day for someone through encouraging words? Sometimes just being in their presence brings such joy. It's usually the little things that really seem to matter to people: At just the right time there's a telephone call; a warm smile or big hug; a comforting or positive word when a person is feeling downhearted, rejected, unloved and discouraged; or even a silly little joke to make someone laugh. There never was a person born who didn't need a kind word. What makes the difference in the lives of many people—whether they succeed or fail—is the encouraging word of someone else. It might be to someone you pass by every day. God will give you the words to encourage them. Encouraging others is a choice we must make because the God whom you and I serve is a God of encouragement.

Eph. 4:29 from the Amplified Bible is a wonderful plumb line for the words we speak. Paul exhorts us to *"Let no foul or polluting language, nor evil word nor unwholesome or worthless talk [ever] come out of your mouth, but only such [speech] as is good and beneficial to the spiritual progress of others, as is fitting to the need and the occasion, that it may be a blessing and give grace (God's favor) to those who hear it."*

From the New International Version Paul instructs us in I Thess. 5:11-15:

"Therefore encourage one another and build each other up, just as in fact you are doing.

Now we ask you, brothers and sisters, to acknowledge those who work hard among you, who care for you in the Lord and who admonish you.

Hold them in the highest regard in love because of their work. Live in peace with each other.

And we urge you, brothers and sisters, warn those who are idle and disruptive, encourage the disheartened, help the weak, be patient with everyone.

Make sure that nobody pays back wrong for wrong, but always strive to do what is good for each other...and for everyone else."

What exactly is encouragement? One dictionary defines it "to give courage or confidence to; to raise the hopes of; to help on by sympathetic advice and interest, to advise and make it easy for someone to do something, to promote or stimulate and to strengthen."

In contrast discouragement is "to say or take

away the courage of, to deter, to lessen enthusiasm for and so restrict or hinder, depression, dejection, things that discourages and brings hopelessness.

Amazingly, our words have the capacity to do both and we are faced with the choice every time we speak as to which it will be. I think we could all agree that many times we should have said such words as: Thanks for a job well done; thanks for all you do; you're much loved; I greatly appreciate you; how can I pray for you today; you look lovely or handsome but regretfully those words were never spoken. (1)

God has given us an incredible treasure – the gift of words. But the gift wasn't meant to be hoarded or ill-used. The gift is to be opened and shared to help others be all that God intended them to be. (2)

Offering encouragement is so much more than saying a few nice words, it is a gift that can literally transform people and circumstances.

Miss Thompson, a school teacher who taught fifth grade, saw firsthand how an encouraging word can change the course of a day, the course of a life. Here's her story in her own words. It's very touching so you may need to get your Kleenex out. The title of the story is *"Three Letters from Teddy."*

"Teddy's letter came today and now that I've read it, I will place it in my cedar chest with the other things that are important to my life.

"I wanted you to be the first to know."

I smiled as I read the words he had written, and my heart swelled with a pride that I had no right to feel. I have not seen Teddy Stallard since he was a student in my fifth-grade class, fifteen years ago.

I'm ashamed to say that from the first day he stepped into my classroom, I disliked Teddy. Teachers try hard not to have favorites in a class, but we try even harder not to show dislike for a child, any child.

Nevertheless, every year there are one or two children that one cannot help but be attached to, for teachers are human, and it is human nature to like bright, pretty, intelligent people, whether they are ten years old or twenty-five. And sometimes, not too often fortunately, there will be one or two students to whom the teacher just can't seem to relate.

I had thought myself capable of handling my personal feelings along that line until Teddy walked into my life. There wasn't a child I particularly liked that year, but Teddy was most assuredly one I disliked.

He was a dirty little boy. Not just occasionally, but all the time. His hair hung low over his ears, *and he actually had to hold it out of his eyes as he wrote his papers in class. (And this was before it was fashionable to do so!) Too, he had a peculiar odor about him that I could never identify. Yes, his physical faults were many, but his intellect left a lot to be desired. By the end of the first week I knew he was hopelessly behind the others. Not only was he behind, he was just plain slow! I began to withdraw from him immediately. Any teacher will tell you that it's more of a pleasure to teach a bright child. It is definitely more rewarding for one's ego. But any teacher worth his or her credentials can channel work to the bright child, keeping that child challenged and learning, while the major effort is with the slower ones.*

Any teacher can do this. Most teachers do, but I didn't. Not that year. In fact, I concentrated on many best students and let the others follow along as best they could. Ashamed as I am to admit it, I took perverse pleasure in using my red pen; and each time I came to Teddy's papers, the cross-marks (and they were many) were always a little larger and a little redder than necessary. "Poor work!" I would write with a flourish.

While I did not actually ridicule the boy, my attitude was obviously quite apparent to the class, for he quickly became the class "goat," the outcast – the unlovable and the unloved. He knew I didn't like him, but he didn't know why. Nor did I know-

then or now-why I felt such an intense dislike for him. All I know is that he was a little boy no one cared about, and I made no effort on his behalf.

The days rolled by and we made it through the Fall Festival, the Thanksgiving holidays, and I continued marking happily with my red pen. As our Christmas break approached, I knew that Teddy would never catch up in time to be promoted to the sixth-grade level. He would be a repeater.

To justify myself, I went to his cumulative folder from time to time. He had very low grades for the first four years, but no grade failure. How he had made it, I didn't know. I closed my mind to the personal remarks

First grade: "Teddy shows promise by work and attitude, but he has a poor home situation."

Second grade: "Teddy could do better. Mother terminally ill. He receives little help at home."

Third grade: "Teddy is a pleasant boy. Helpful, but too serious. Slow learner. Mother passed away end of the year."

Fourth grade: "Very slow but well behaved. Father shows no interest."

Well, they passed him four times, but he will certainly repeat fifth grade! Do him good! I said to myself. And then the last day before the holidays arrived. Our little tree on the reading table sported *paper and popcorn chains. Many gifts were heaped underneath, waiting for the big moment. Teachers always get several gifts at Christmas, but mine that year seemed bigger and more elaborate than ever. There was not a student who had not brought me one. Each unwrapping brought squeals of delight and the proud giver would receive effusive thank-you's. His gift wasn't the last one I picked up. In fact it was in the middle of the pile. Its wrapping was a brown paper bag, and he had colored Christmas trees and red bells all over it. It was stuck together with masking tape. "For Miss Thompson – From Teddy." The group was completely silent and I felt conspicuous, embarrassed because they all stood watching me unwrap that gift. As I removed the last bit of masking tape, two items fell to my desk. A gaudy rhinestone bracelet with several stones missing and a small bottle of dime-store cologne- half empty. I could hear the snickers and whispers, and I wasn't sure I could look at Teddy. "Isn't this lovely?" I asked, placing the bracelet on my wrist. "Teddy, would you help me fasten it?"*

He smiled shyly as he fixed the clasp, and I held up my wrist for all of them to admire. There were a few hesitant ooh's and ahh's, but, as I dabbed the cologne behind my ears, all the little girls lined up for a dab behind their ears. I continued to open the gifts until I reached the bottom of the pile. We ate our refreshments until the bell rang. The children filed out with shouts of "See you next year!" and "Merry Christmas!" but Teddy waited at his desk.

When they had all left, he walked toward me clutching his gift and books to his chest. "You smell just like Mom," he said softly. "Her bracelet looks real pretty on you, too. I'm glad you liked it."

He left quickly and I locked the door, sat down at my desk and wept, resolving to make up to Teddy what I had deliberately deprived him of a teacher who cared.

I stayed every afternoon with Teddy from the day class resumed on January 2 until the last day of school. Sometimes we worked together. Sometimes he worked alone while I drew up lesson plans or graded papers. Slowly but surely he caught up with the rest of the class.

Gradually there was a definite upward curve in his grades. He did not have to repeat the fifth grade. In fact, his final averages were among the highest in the class, and although I knew he would be moving out of the state when school was out, I was not worried for him.

Teddy had reached a level that would stand him in good stead the following year, no matter where he went. He had enjoyed a measure of success and as we were taught in our education courses: "Success builds success." I did not hear from Teddy until several years later when his first letter appeared in my mailbox.

Dear Miss Thompson,

I just wanted you to be the first to know. I will be graduating second in my class on May 25th from my High School.

Very truly yours,

Teddy Stallard

I sent him a card of congratulations and a small package, a pen and pencil set. I wondered what he would do after graduation. I found out four years later when Teddy's second letter came.

Dear Miss Thompson,

I was just informed today that I'll be graduating first in my class.

The university has been a little tough but I'll miss it.

Very truly yours,

Teddy Stallard

I sent him a good pair of sterling silver monogrammed cuff links and a card, so proud of him I could burst!

And now—today—Teddy's third letter:

Dear Miss Thompson,

I wanted you to be the first to know. As of today I am Theodore J.

Stallard, MD. How about that????!!!!

I'm going to be married on July 27, and I'm hoping you can come and sit where Mom would sit if she were here. I'll have no family

there as Dad died last year.

Very truly yours,

Ted Stallard

I'm not sure what kind of gift one sends to a doctor on completion of medical school. Maybe I'll just wait and take a wedding gift, but the note can't wait.

Dear Ted,

Congratulations! You made it and you did it yourself! In spite of those like me and not because of us, this day has come for you.

God bless you. I'll be at that wedding with bells on!!!

Miss Thompson changed the course of one little boy's life. She gave Teddy words that built him up when he felt as though life had knocked him down for good. Can't you hear her now? "Great job, Teddy!" "You can do it!"

She became the wind beneath his wings when he felt as though he had been grounded from flight. And years later, she had a front row seat as she watched him soar into his future. That is the power of a person's words. An incredible gift God has given those created in His very image. (3)

How long do words linger in someone's heart? How far-reaching are the echoes of a kind, encouraging word? I believe the impact of a spoken or written word can remain long after our bodies have left this earth. Marie learned the lasting impact of words from a group of her students. Here is her story:

He was in the first third-grade class I taught at Saint Mary's School in Morris, Minnesota. All thirty-four of my students were dear to me, but Mark Eklund was one in a million. Very neat in appearance, he had that happy-to-be-alive attitude that made even his occasional mischievousness delightful.

Mark also talked incessantly. I had to remind him again and again that talking without permission was not acceptable. What impressed me so much, though, was his sincere response every time I had to correct him for misbehaving. "Thank you for correcting me, Sister!" I didn't know what to make of it at first, but before long I became accustomed to hearing it many times a day.

One morning my patience was growing thin when Mark talked once too often, and then I made a novice-teacher's mistake. I looked at Mark and said, "If you say one more word, I am going to tape your mouth shut!" It wasn't ten seconds later when Chuck blurted out, "Mark is talking again." I hadn't asked any of the students to help me watch Mark, but since I had stated the punishment in front of the class, I had to act on it.

I remember the scene as if it had occurred this morning. I walked to my desk, very deliberately opened the drawer, and took out a roll of masking tape. Without saying a word, I proceeded to Mark's desk, tore off two pieces of tape and made a big X with them over his mouth. I then returned to the front of the room.

As I glanced at Mark to see how he was doing, he winked at me. That did it! I started laughing. The class cheered as I walked back to Mark's desk, removed the tape, and shrugged my shoulders. His first words were, "Thank you for correcting me, Sister."

At the end of the year I was asked to teach

junior high math. The years flew by, and before I knew it Mark was in my classroom again. He was more handsome than ever and just as polite. Since he had to listen carefully to my instruction in the "new math," he did not talk as much in ninth grade as he had in the third.

One Friday, things just didn't feel right. We had worked hard on a new concept all week, and I sensed that the students were growing frustrated with themselves and edgy with one another. I had to stop this crankiness before it got out of hand. So I asked them to list the names of the other students in the room on two sheets of paper, leaving a space between each name. Then I told them to think of the nicest thing they could say about each of their classmates and write it down.

It took the remainder of the class period to finish the assignment, and as the students left the room, each one handed me the papers. Charlie smiled. Mark said, "Thank you for teaching me, Sister. Have a good weekend."

That Saturday, I wrote down the name of each student on a separate sheet of paper, and I listed what everyone else had said about that individual. On Monday I gave each student his or her list. Before long, the entire class was smiling. "Really?" I heard whispered. "I never knew that meant anything to anyone!" "I didn't know others liked me so much!"

No one ever mentioned those papers in class again. I never knew if they discussed them after class or with their parents, but it didn't matter. The exercise had accomplished its purpose. The students were happy with themselves and with one another again.

That group of students moved on. Several years later, after I returned from vacation, my parents met me at the airport. As we were driving home, Mother asked the usual questions about the trip, the weather, and my experiences in general. There was a slight lull in the conversation. Mother gave Dad a sideways glance and simply said, "Dad?" My father cleared his throat as he usually did before something important. "The Eklunds called last night," he began. "Really?" I said. "I haven't heard from them in years. I wonder how Mark is."

Dad responded quietly. "Mark was killed in Vietnam," he said. "The funeral is tomorrow, and his parents would like it if you could attend." To this day I can still point to the exact spot on I-494 where Dad told me about Mark.

I had never seen a serviceman in a military coffin before. Mark looked so handsome, so mature. All I could think at that moment was Mark, I would give all the masking tape in the world if only you would talk to me.

The church was packed with Mark's friends. Chuck's sister sang "The Battle Hymn of the Republic." Why did it have to rain on the day of the funeral? It was difficult enough at the graveside. The pastor said the usual prayers, and the bugler played "Taps." One by one those who loved Mark took a last walk by the coffin.

I was the last one. As I stood there, one of the soldiers who had acted as pallbearer came up to me. "Were you Mark's math teacher?" He asked. I nodded as I continued to stare at the coffin. "Mark talked about you a lot," he said.

After the funeral, most of Mark's former classmates headed to Chuck's farmhouse for lunch. Mark's mother and father were there, obviously waiting for me. "We want to show you something," his father said, taking a wallet out of his pocket. "They found this on Mark when he was killed. We thought you might recognize it."

Opening the billfold, he carefully removed two worn pieces of notebook paper that had obviously been taped, folded, and refolded many times. I knew without looking that the papers were the ones on which I had listed all the good things each of Mark's classmates had said about him. "Thank you so much for that," Mark's mother said. "As you can see, Mark treasured it." Mark's classmates started to gather around us. Charlie smiled rather sheepishly and said, "I still have my list. It's in the top drawer of my desk at home." Chuck's wife said, "Chuck asked me to put his in our wedding album." "I have mine too," Marilyn said. "It's in my diary." Then Vicki, another classmate, reached into her pocketbook, took out her wallet, and showed her worn and frazzled list to the group. "I carry this with me at all times," Vicki said without batting an eyelash. "I think we all saved our lists."

How long will our words echo in the hearts and minds of our children, our husbands, our friends, fellow believers, and the world? For all eternity, my friends. To the end of the age. (4)

In some ways the impact of our words can change people's concept of us, others, of themselves, and ultimately of God. What an awesome responsibility all of us have to guard well what comes out of our mouths. Words can hurt. They are characterized in scripture as arrows, darts, daggers and swords. If these powerful instruments are wielded in the wrong way, they can cut, stab, leaving wounds that may never heal, scars that can last a lifetime. They can even kill.

In Prov. 12:18 from the Tree of Life Version it says *"reckless speech is like the thrusts of a sword, but the tongue of the wise brings healing."*

Washington Irving said, "A sharp tongue is the only edged-tool that grows keener with constant use." (5)

Someone has said, "Many have fallen by the edge of the sword but not so many as have fallen by the tongue."

Words can alienate, isolate, divide families, and destroy relationships and reputations. Words can spread misery and bring much hurt, grief and pain. They can emotionally cripple others or they can bring encouragement, healing, restoration and reconciliation.

The painful words often are the ones remembered longer and carried deeper, in places so deep and dark that no one can ever reach them. Only those words, spoken from a loving heart with the kind words that only Jesus can inspire, will ever reach those broken pieces of the human heart.

The Apostle Paul tells us that some of the purposes of prophecy are for people to be strengthened, encouraged and comforted.

I Cor. 14:3-4 from the New Living Translation says, *"But one who prophesies is helping others grow in the Lord, encouraging and comforting them. A person who speaks in tongues is strengthened personally in the Lord, but one who speaks a word of prophecy strengthens the entire church."*

Perhaps the most famous encourager in

scripture is Barnabas, whose name actually means "son of encouragement."

Interestingly, his name also means "son of the prophet."

While we don't see any prophetic words from Barnabas recorded in the book of Acts, we do see him stepping out in faith and what could even be considered prophetic pacts all flowing from a desire to encourage and build people up in their faith.

As we seek to grow in our ability to encourage others, think about the weight and significance of this!

When you encourage someone, you are imparting to them the ability to face their challenge, risk, pain, etc. Without being crippled by fear. You are infusing their hearts with the courage to move forward.

What an amazing privilege and responsibility God has entrusted us with. (7)

Before ending this chapter, I must tell you something about a very vital element of the importance of always speaking loving, caring and encouraging words to avoid those painful regrets in life.

One can accumulate many regrets over a life time for not sharing enough of those precious, priceless moments with family, friends and special loved ones like we should have.

No one ever wished they had spent more time at the office, or wished that they had taken more alcohol to drink at the bar they frequented, instead of being home with their families - where they should have been to begin with.

Poor choices always result in unpleasant consequences and regrets that can last for many years and even a life time.

They leave a permanent scar not only on your *own* heart, but on the hearts of those we never meant to hurt. But whether we meant to or not, we did.

Sadly, most of us as we age and mature would almost give anything to take back those angry words we've spoken that were harsh, unkind, and hurtful especially to our family! Words that we wish we hadn't said that has caused us painful regrets.

What is regret?

Webster's Dictionary defines regret as a troubled feeling or remorse over something that has happened, especially over something that one has done or left undone.

'The Exploding Dictionary' on the web gives another definition. It says it's 'pain of mind on account of something done or experienced in the past, with a wish that it had been different; a looking back with dissatisfaction or with longing; grief; sorrow; especially, a mourning on account of the loss of some joy, advantage, or satisfaction.'

In general regrets may also result from guilt: bad things we've done, or good things we have *failed* to do. It also results in shame that produces bad feelings about who we are.

The death of an important person in our life can leave us with some unfinished business.

Something we wish we had said or done before they died but never took the time to do so.

I heard a story of a woman who had been very ugly to her bedridden mother over something very petty.

She left her mother's home, leaving the poor old woman in tears over her behavior. She said a lot of hurtful things about her poor, sick old Mother.

She blamed everyone else for what happened that day, and decided she was going to "punish" her mother by not having any contact with her.

She figured her Mother would beg her to come back.

The next time she saw her mother, the old woman was lying in a casket at her funeral.

This woman was so overcome with guilt that she turned her back on her younger sister, and couldn't even bear to look at her mother's body.

It was too late for any apologies, or loving words. It was too late for anything, except for guilt, regret and pain.

Stop and think for a moment. Have you ever wished you had just a piece of yesterday back – just a tiny piece – to speak one more time to someone who passed away?

I've learned over the years that you should treat a person kindly today, for the people we love the most are often taken away from us too soon.

Are there things you wish you had said to your departed parents? A brother or sister you've lost?

An affectionate grandmother you never thanked?

There's many moments in our lives that we'd like to live over, to do them over and do better or do right, but that's not possible.

Few things are more painful in life than from a sense of regret felt for things done or things not done!

So to avoid any more regrets in your life, I would encourage you not to wait until a person is on their death bed or has passed away to make regular contact with them when you can either by letter, email, text, telephone or preferably in person.

So how do we gain freedom from the painful over-whelming regrets of guilt and shame?

No one likes to feel guilty. Like an unwelcome guest, guilt shows up at the worst possible time and does not go away no matter how much you wish it would.

Yet the truth is that we need guilt. It is the only proper response to any offense, whether a selfish thought or a premeditated murder. Even a nonbeliever wants a burglar to feel remorse for his theft.

Why? Because he *should.*

Guilt exposes the truth that we wish to avoid: We have all sinned.

Romans 3:23-25 declares:

"for all have sinned and fall short of the glory of God, being justified freely by His grace through the redemption that is in Christ Jesus, whom God set forth as a propitiation by His blood, through faith, to demonstrate His righteousness, because in His forbearance God had passed over the sins that were previously committed, to demonstrate at the present time His righteousness, that He might be just and the justifier of the one who has faith in Jesus.

All have sinned and no one can live up to what

God created us to be; we all fall short of His glory.

We cannot save ourselves because as sinners we can never meet God's requirements. Our only hope is through faith in Jesus Christ.

John puts it this way In First John 1:5-8:

"This is the message which we have heard from Him and declare to you, that God is light and in Him is no darkness at all. If we say that we have fellowship with Him, and walk in darkness, we lie and do not practice the truth. But if we walk in the light as He is in the light, we have fellowship with one another, and the blood of Jesus Christ His Son cleanses us from all sin. If we say that we have no sin, we deceive ourselves, and the truth is not in us."

But John does not leave us with this dismal picture of ourselves. Instead he goes on to paint a glorious portrait of a forgiving God.

First John 1:9 and 10 says: *"If we confess our sins, He is faithful and just to forgive us our sins and to cleanse us from all unrighteousness. If we say that we have not sinned, we make Him a liar, and His word is not in us."*

Only the Blood of Jesus Christ can cleanse us from all sin, making it possible for imperfect believers to have fellowship with a Holy God.

Guilt does more than just deliver the distressing news. It unlocks the door to forgiveness. Progress, change, reform, and (most important of all) God's forgiveness all start with confession.

Confession works against the worst part of human nature, the part that imagines itself to be better than it really is.

What person has not felt, and at times verbalized, "I'm not perfect, but I'm not as bad as my next-door neighbor"?

This mindset always stops short of confessing; it would rather ignore or ease feelings of guilt than admit them.

But only open confession of our sins will completely cleanse us. Only when we admit that we are sinners, unworthy of God's grace, can we make a fresh start.

C.S. Lewis said that "no man knows how bad he is till he has tried very hard to be good."

I have a very good friend who used to work in police work and the jails.

She said she always knew when someone was telling the truth about their involvement in a crime – or if they told ALL the truth of their involvement in a crime – by their actions.

When they were lying, or hadn't told everything, they paced, they sweated, they cursed and probably walked miles around and around their jail cells.

But once they had told everything they knew, when they had admitted their involvement, and had told the complete truth, they would lay down in the cell and sleep like a baby.

The truth may not have freed them from the jail cell, but it freed their conscience.

To quote the author, Michael Morgan, "There is no greater prison than the one within."

Similarly, we can never know how much we need freedom until we try to unload our burden of sin. Yet God's forgiveness will liberate us to begin anew on the path of righteousness. (6)

Without the forgiveness and peace from God, I don't know how some people could live with their guilt. And, in fact, some don't.

People have lost their sanity and even their lives because they were drowned under their guilt and shame. Many suicides occur because the person just doesn't know of any other way to ease their very heavy burden of guilt.

But for Christians, God can give us not only peace but can help us make amends when appropriate.

This doesn't mean we get a "free pass" from God when we have done something wrong.

Too often, Christians take the attitude, "Well, God forgives me, so I don't have to do anything."

Not true!

Jesus Himself teaches His disciples about the process of restoring an erring believer in a loving personal confrontation to be reconciled.

Jesus says in Mt. 5:23-24:

"Therefore if you bring your gift to the altar, and there remember that your brother has something against you, leave your gift there before the altar, and go your way. First be reconciled to your brother, and then come and offer your gift."

If the other party won't accept our apologies, that's on them. But we are required to try.

In Mt. 18:15-17 Jesus also deals with a sinning brother and says:

"Moreover if your brother sins against you, go and tell him his fault between you and him alone. If he hears you, you have gained your brother. But if he will not hear, take with you one or two more, that 'by the mouth of two or three witnesses every word may be established.' And if he refuses to hear them, tell it to the church. But if he refuses even to hear the church, let him be to you like a heathen and a tax collector."

While we may have to live with earthly consequences of what led to our regrets, God will give us grace and even bring good from those mistakes.

Romans 8:28 says: *"And we know that all things work together for good to those who love God, to those who are the called according to His purpose."*

Here are some further scriptures to help encourage you to gain freedom from the regrets of guilt and shame.

In Eph. 1:7-8 The Apostle Paul says of Jesus,

"In Him we have redemption through His blood, the forgiveness of sins, according to the riches of His grace."

The word redemption means "buy back" or "ransom." In ancient times, one could buy back a person who was sold into slavery. In the same way, Christ through His death bought us from slavery to sin.

The blood of Christ is the means by which our redemption comes. The Old Testament and the New both clearly teach that there is no forgiveness without the shedding of Blood.

Blood here is a vivid, symbolic equivalent to death. It recalls the sacrificial system of the Old Covenant, which looked forward to the self-sacrifice of Jesus Christ that took away the sins of the world.

In Psa. 32:1-6 entitled "The Joy of Forgiveness", where David finally admits his failures and says:

Blessed is he whose transgression is forgiven, Whose sin is covered. Blessed is the man to whom the LORD does not impute iniquity, And in whose spirit there is no deceit.

When I kept silent, my bones grew old Through my groaning all the day long. For day and night Your hand was heavy upon me; My vitality was turned into the drought of summer. Selah
I acknowledged my sin to You, And my iniquity I have not hidden. I said, "I will confess my transgressions to the LORD," And You forgave the iniquity of my sin. Selah

For this cause everyone who is godly shall pray to You In a time when You may be found;

Surely in a flood of great waters

They shall not come near him.

The silence of David was a stubborn resistance to admitting guilt, a hope that in time the sin and its penalty would go away.

The more David delayed his confession, the more he suffered. David realized it was not just his conscience or his feelings that were assaulting him, but the heavy hand of God.

No matter who else is hurt, the principal offense of any sin is always against the Lord.

The consequences of David's sin with

Bathsheba remained despite God's forgiveness. But at this point, the greater news was God's forgiveness. God had restored his relationship with David.

In Psa. 51:1-4 David said:

Have mercy upon me, O God According to Your loving kindness; According to the multitude of Your tender mercies, Blot out my transgressions. Wash me thoroughly from my iniquity, And cleanse me from my sin.

For I acknowledge my transgressions, And my sin is always before me. Against You, You only, have I sinned, And done this evil in Your sight-

That You may be found just when You speak, And blameless when You judge.

The months of agony that David suffered because of His guilt are expressed in the striking words – **my sin is always before me**.

In Psalm 103:1-5 the Psalmist David said in his Psalm of Praise:

Bless the LORD, O my soul; And all that is within me, bless His holy name! Bless the LORD, O my soul, And forget not all His benefits: Who forgives all your iniquities, Who heals all your diseases, Who redeems your life from destruction, Who crowns you with lovingkindness and tender mercies, Who satisfies your mouth with good things, So that your youth is renewed like the eagle's.

In Heb. 8:12 God promised in His New Covenant:

"For I will be merciful to their unrighteousness, and their sins and their lawless deeds I will remember no more."

Psa. 103:12 says:

"As far as the east is from the west, So far has He removed our transgressions from us."

Micah 7:18-19 says:

"Who is a God like You, Pardoning iniquity And passing over the transgression of the remnant of His heritage?

He does not retain His anger forever, Because He delights in mercy. He will again have compassion on us, And will subdue our iniquities.

You will cast all our sins Into the depths of the sea."

It is often humorously said that God casts our sins into the depths of the sea of His forgetfulness and puts up a sign: "No fishing allowed!"

However, Satan can use guilt feelings to rob us of our joy and effectiveness for Christ. Often he brings to our remembrance the past with all its ugliness.

To overcome this assault, we must have full assurance that we have been forgiven of our sin.

Then we must dwell with Christ in daily communion, constantly aware of His glory and the joy of knowing that He wants to use us *in spite* of our past.

Henry T. Blackaby, the author of <u>*Experiencing God*</u>, said, "God does not call the qualified; He qualifies the called."

Having received forgiveness in Christ, we must next forgive ourselves for our failures.

This is what I believe the apostle Paul was thinking when he wrote in Phil. 3:13, *"Brethren, I do not count myself to have apprehended; but one thing I do, forgetting those things which are behind and reaching forward to those things which are ahead."*

Author Jeff Wickfield eloquently stated on this issue, "Why do you think the windshield is so much bigger than the rear view mirror?

Because it's more important to see where you're going than where you've been."

I picture Paul sitting down one day and, in a state of despair, declaring, "I am the worst of sinners."

Then the Holy Spirit whispers, "forget those things which are behind. You did your best. You did all that you could do, and God knows all about it, so forget all the things which are behind you as

Paul said in Phil. 3:14, *"I press toward the goal for the prize of the upward call of God in Christ Jesus."*

The goal in this scripture specifically refers to the marker at the end of a race on which runners intently fix their eyes.

The prize is the reward for victory.

The upward call speaks of the divine call to complete salvation. It may also refer to the judgement seat of Christ. The place of reward.

Paul does not say that he is pressing on for the call of God but rather for the prize of that call. He is not working for his salvation but rather for a reward for his faithfulness.

The Lord deals with sin in two ways: the wicked receive God's just condemnation; and the righteous receives His undeserved mercy.

Romans 8:1-11 says:

"There is therefore now no condemnation to those who are in Christ Jesus, who do not walk according to the flesh, but according to the Spirit.

For the law of the Spirit of life in Christ Jesus has made me free from the law of sin and death. For what the law could not do in that it was weak through the flesh, God did by sending His own Son in the likeness of sinful flesh, on account of sin: He condemned sin in the flesh, that the righteous requirement of the law might be fulfilled in us who do not walk according to the flesh but according to the Spirit

For those who live according to the flesh set their minds on the things of the flesh, but those who live according to the Spirit, the things of the Spirit.

For to be carnally minded is death, but to be spiritually minded is life and peace. Because the carnal mind is enmity against God; for it is not subject to the law of God, nor indeed can be. So then, those who are in the flesh cannot please God.

But you are not in the flesh but in the Spirit, if indeed the Spirit of God dwells in you. Now if anyone does not have the Spirit of Christ, he is not His.

And if Christ is in you, the body is dead because of sin, but the Spirit is life because of righteousness. But if the Spirit of Him who raised Jesus from the dead dwells in you, He who raised Christ from the dead will also give life to your mortal bodies through His Spirit who dwells in you."

After reading this chapter, it would be good for you to offer up to God this declaration of prayer:

Thank you Jesus for forgiving all my sins!

I boldly declare that I am forgiven, that I have been made the righteousness of God.

That there is now no condemnation for me because I am completely forgiven!

Amen

One of my favorite scriptures in the Bible given to us by God that is so very comforting is found in Jer. 29:11 that says:

"For I know the thoughts that I think toward you, says The Lord, thoughts of peace and not of evil, to give you a future and a hope."

Even though these words were spoken to the nation of Israel over twenty-five hundred years ago, they apply to every one of us today, to every person who is a child of God. And that includes you!

CHAPTER 7

IS YOUR SPEECH MOTIVATED BY THE WISDOM AND LOVE OF GOD?

Wisdom is knowing when to speak your mind and when to mind your speech. Wisdom is the foundation of good communication because:

1) Wisdom enlightens us that speaking wisely is nothing more than making a series of good choices! It enables us to choose our words, our responses, and our listening style with care.

2) Wisdom signals we listen to the "third voice" in every conversation. We stay tuned to the Holy Spirit's voice. We walk closely to God and let that closeness inform how we communicate and

3) We experience less stress, more sleep, and

a deep sense of well-being from life lived well – because of Wisdom.

Communication is the foundation of everything we have with each other. There is really nothing we do more frequently than communicate. Speaking wisely is based on being a person of deep, genuine, God-inspired—ultimate—love! "Love one another" is the new commandment Jesus gave repeatedly in the gospel of John. He didn't say you "should." He didn't say "I want you to." He said, "Do it." There is no room for debate. It isn't an option, suggestion or recommendation. It is a commandment. It is one of God's Laws.

In John 13:34, 35 Jesus said, *"A new commandment I give you that you love one another as I have loved you that you also love one another by this all will know that you are my disciples if you have love for one another."*

In John 15:17 Jesus also said, *"These things I command you, that you love one another."*

When the Apostle Paul started his essay on love in I Cor. 13 the first element he talks about is speech. Particularly in the way we deal with each other. He indicates that while speech may be eloquent and impressive, if it's not rooted and grounded in love, the result is empty and meaningless. Love is how we're going to change the world.

In I Cor. 13:1-8 and verse 13 called the Love Chapter Paul declares *"Though I speak with the tongues of men and of angels, but have not love, I have become sounding brass or a clanging cymbal. And though I have the gift of prophecy, and understand all mysteries and all knowledge, and though I have all faith, so that I could remove mountains, but have not love, I am nothing. And though I bestow all my goods to feed the poor, and though I give my body to be burned, but have not love, it profits me nothing.*

Love suffers long and is kind; love does not envy; love does not parade itself, is not puffed up; does not behave rudely, does not seek its own, is not provoked, thinks no evil; does not rejoice in iniquity, but rejoices in the truth; bears all things, believes all things, hopes all things, endures all things. Love never fails. But whether there are prophecies, they will fail; whether there are tongues, they will cease; whether there is knowledge, it will vanish away." And finally Vs 13 says *"And now abide faith, hope, love, these three; but the greatest of these is love."*

Calling ourselves Christian doesn't automatically make us loving. Poets and artists have been trying to describe it for centuries but have continually missed the mark. Love is not a feeling; Love is a verb! It's a word of action. We have to decide every day to speak and act in loving ways. We also need to depend on the Spirit of God to guide us into what it means to love as we realize more and more how deeply loved we are by our Creator.

Language can build or destroy relationships. Words can make our lives happy or unhappy. Words can spread a shroud of darkness and misery or forge a chain of grief. Words can create an atmosphere of good or evil. But words are not the only way we communicate. We communicate by the way we react to a problem situation, by the way we respond to the felt or expressed needs of others, and by the nuances of our behavior; such as our tone of voice, eye contact, body language, how well we listen with interest and attentiveness, etc.

Communication is a multifaceted challenge. Love is a language! In fact, it's a language that is unfailing in all ways. All Christian communication must be guided by love.

Communication is composed of many elements, both verbal and nonverbal. The most effective vehicle to convey that language is love. Where there is great love there are always miracles. Love is a language that everybody understands!

CHAPTER 8

WORDS ARE AMONG THE MOST POWERFUL FORCES IN THE UNIVERSE

Now you should all understand that the tongue is used throughout scripture in both literal and metaphorical ways especially in the Psalms, Proverbs and the Book of James. This holds true whether we're speaking of spiritual, physical or emotional "life or death."

Do you fully realize just how important the words you speak are? And I do mean every word that comes out of your mouth. It does not matter if you are speaking to yourselves or to others. As I said before, words are one of the most powerful forces in the universe. The spoken word can bring life or death and you can control them. You can decide both what you say and don't say. God created the world by the power of His words and He has given you the power to bring life or death

75

by the words you choose. What you say or don't say with your tongues can have a profound effect on others more than anyone realizes. What a responsibility!

Wayne Christensen of Fox Lake community Church wrote *"Soft words sung in a lullaby will put a baby to sleep. Excited words will stir a mob to violence. Eloquent words will send armies marching into the face of death. Encouraging words will fan to flame the genius of a Rembrandt or a Lincoln. Powerful words will mold the public mind as the sculptor molds his clay. Words spoken or written are a dynamic force."*

It's no wonder that the apostle called the Scriptures the written word "the Sword of God." Your words are extremely powerful! Your Words are your swords to use in your battle for success and happiness. How others react towards you depends in a large measure upon the words you speak to them.

Life is a great whispering gallery that sends back echoes of the words you send out. Your words live beyond you. They go marching through the years in the lives of all those with whom you will ever come in contact. What you say and how you say it makes a difference in the lives of yourselves and others. That's why taking control of your conversation is so very important.

Stories abound regarding the power of words.

Our words can make a difference between daily victory and daily defeat. They can make or break someone's future. They can even break someone's heart. Words have the power to motivate or destroy, energize or deflate, inspire or create despair. Many successful executives can remember the time their father failed to give affirmation to them as a child. The result was either overachievement to prove their worth or underachievement to prove he was right.

Many wives have lost their ability to love because of critical husbands. Many husbands have left their marriages because of words of disrespect and ungratefulness. However, there are just as many stories of those who have been encouraged, challenged, and comforted with words that made a positive difference in their lives.

Think back for a moment. How many of your troubles could be prevented if you would learn to control your tongues? How much of the heartache you have caused others could have been avoided. If only you would have chosen more thoughtful words to speak! Think about your own life how words have affected you. Did they help? Or hurt? Think about the person who may have told you or someone else with putdowns like: you were ugly or stupid, you were incompetent, could never do anything right, or that you would never amount to anything.

Every person who has been married knows what it is like to say the wrong thing at the wrong time. Careless statements can provoke or escalate a conflict. But it's not only in marriage it's in any tense situation where words can either diffuse anger, or pour gasoline on the fire of conflict.

Angry, sharp, aggressive and critical words cause barriers and defenses to go up. These kinds of words make you feel attacked and when you feel attacked you most often strike back, attempting to hurt the other person as much or worse than they hurt you. Sarcasm, insults and accusations, inevitably cause conflict to escalate, whether it ends up in broken relationships or world wars.

On the other hand soft words, kind words, gentle and understanding words can diffuse even the most hostile situation. Words that convey calm, peace, and maybe even concern and love; that lead to productive conversation.

Words are powerful and can destroy a person's life.

Prov. 11:9-11 says, *"The hypocrite with his mouth destroys his neighbor, But through knowledge the righteous will be delivered. When it goes well with the righteous, the city rejoices; And when the wicked perish, there is jubilation. By the blessing of the upright the city is exalted, But it is overthrown by the mouth of the wicked."*

I wonder how many people, perhaps including you, have had their reputation tarnished or ruined by a lie or how many marriages have been put at risk, or destroyed, by false accusations and innuendos? How many friends have been "thrown under the bus" so that someone could protect a lie? How many spirits have been crushed on a job by a mean-spirited comment and that person has stopped working hard because someone failed to encourage or thank them?

Words can destroy a reputation; they can destroy a person's business; and it can destroy their witness in their walk with the Lord. Have you heard the Karen Carpenter story? Karen was part of a singing duo called "The Carpenters." They had many hit records that are still played often on some of the "oldie" stations. Karen died unexpectedly of heart failure at age 32 brought on by years of self-abuse from the eating disorder anorexia nervosa. But what was it that brought on Karen's fatal obsession with weight control? USA Today reported that it all started when a reviewer once called her "Richard's chubby sister."

The following is a very sad story because of misspoken words and lack of encouragement.

Gary Inrig tells of some parents on the East Coast who got a telephone call from their son during the Korean War. They were thrilled, because they hadn't heard from him for many months. He said he was in San Francisco on his way home. The son said, "Mom, I just wanted to let you know that I'm bringing a buddy home with me. He got hurt pretty bad and he only has one eye, one arm, and one leg. I'd sure like him to live with us." "Sure son," his mother replied. "He sounds like a brave man. We can find room for him for a while." "Mom, you don't understand. I want him to come and live with us." "Well, okay," she finally said. "We could try it for six months or so." "No mom, I want him to stay always. He needs us. He's only got one eye, one arm and one leg. He's really in bad shape."

By now the mother had lost her patience. "Son, you're being unrealistic about this. You're emotional because you've been in a war. That boy will be a drag on you and a constant problem for all of us. Be reasonable." The phone clicked dead. The next day the parents got a telegram: their son committed suicide. A week later the parents received the body. They looked down with unspeakable sorrow on the corpse of their son who had one eye, one arm, and one leg." (1)

CHAPTER 9

TIMING IS EVERYTHING.

You may have heard the old adage, "Timing is everything." Well according to the Bible...good timing applies to our words and speech too. In the delicate matter of human communication timing is all important. The timing of your words includes spoken and unspoken words. That is when to speak up and when to be silent.

Even though the cardinal scriptural rule for communication is to stop talking and start listening, there obviously comes a time when we must speak. This chapter suggests that when we must speak, we should do so only after contemplating the implication of our words; we should think about our answers before we give them.

That truth seems so self-evident we may

wonder if it is necessary to emphasize it at all. We have only to remember the oft-repeated lament, "I said it before I thought," to understand the strong scriptural indictment of the person who speaks in haste.

Proverbs 29:20 says, *"Do you see a man hasty in his words? There is more hope for a fool than for him."* Even a wise person may become foolish by speaking too quickly. It is better to be silent or choose words carefully than to speak whatever first comes to mind.

As one of our main texts for this teaching says in Eccles. 3:7 *"there is a time to keep silence and a time to speak."* Sometimes silence is the best response to a false charge; at other times, we must speak up. Silence was often the Lord Jesus' way in the face of severe provocation from false witnesses, this is seen in Mt. 26:63; Mk. 14:61 and Mk. 15:4, 5. Defending Himself would have been useless.

Furthermore, He was fulfilling the prophecy of Is 53:7 which states: *He was oppressed and He was afflicted, yet He opened not His mouth; He was led as a lamb to the slaughter, and as a sheep before its shearers is silent, so He opened not His mouth.*

But earlier in His ministry, Jesus rebuked the Pharisees in John 8:13-59 challenging them to prove that He sinned.

When tempted to deride, belittle, or slander a neighbor. Solomon said that it is wise to hold our tongue, recognizing the appropriate time for silence. Prov. 10:18-21 declares, *"Whoever hides hatred has lying lips, and whoever spreads slander is a fool. In the multitude of words sin is not lacking. But he who restrains his lips is wise. The tongue of the righteous is choice silver; the heart of the wicked is worth little. The lips of the righteous feed many, but fools die for lack of wisdom."*

These verses tell of the dangers of speech, particularly lying and slander. The way to avoid these sins is to exercise restraint.

The point of Verse 19 is that words can be so dangerous that we're wiser to not speak than to speak too much while Verse 20 contrasts the speech of those with a right heart which is like silver against those whose heart is far from God and worthless.

And finally Verse 21 describes how proper speech can be like food to the soul. In all these sayings we are challenged to carefully consider how we speak.

Prov. 11:12, 13 says, *"By the blessing of the upright the city is exalted, but it is overthrown by the mouth of the wicked. He who is devoid of wisdom despises his neighbor, but a man of* understanding holds his peace."

When talkativeness or anger tempts us to sin against God or another human being resistance comes by being slow to speak. James urged his fellow believers in James 1:19: *"So then my beloved brethren, let every man be swift to hear, slow to speak, slow to wrath."* The NIV says it this way: *"My dear brothers, take note of this: everyone should be quick to listen, slow to speak and slow to become angry.*

But usually in our conversation with others we reverse that order we are quick to speak and slow to listen. Television's famous Judge Judy paraphrases it beautifully when she says "God gave you two ears and one mouth for a reason. You need to put on your listening ears."

I reiterate, God didn't give us one mouth and two ears for nothing. Perhaps that's a clue that we should listen twice as much as we speak.

Prov. 18:13 says, *"He who answers a matter before he hears it, it is folly and shame to him."* The NIV puts it this way: *"He who answers before listening—that is his folly and his shame."*

Sometimes just a minute of listening in silence can be worth more than an hour of speaking. Years ago an anonymous writer penned a short poem about the merits of measuring our words. *"A wise old owl sat in an oak; the more he saw the less he spoke; the less he spoke the more he heard why can't we all be like that wise old bird?"* (1)

Eccles. 5:2 declares, *"Do not be rash with your mouth, And let not your heart utter anything hastily before God. For God is in heaven, and you on earth; Therefore let your words be few."*

Prov. 26:4, 5 speaks of two contrary ways of responding to a fool when dealing with speaking up or keeping silent. Vs 4 says, *"Do not answer a fool according to his folly, Lest you also be like him."* Vs 5 reads, *"Answer a fool according to his folly, Lest he be wise in his own eyes."*

Some people have called the two Proverbs here contradictory but that is not the case. The phrase "according to his folly" appears twice as a play on words with two shades of meaning. On the one hand, it means by being silent you "avoid the temptation to stoop to his level" that is, don't use his methods, lest you also be like him. On the other hand, it means when you speak up you "avoid the temptation to ignore him altogether" that is, respond in some way, or else he will become wise in his own eyes and his folly will get worse.

As Christians you must learn that there will be times when it is right to boldly and courageously let your voices be heard, rather than looking the other way and not getting involved. It is our duty to speak out on matters of compromising your convictions when confronted with things like gossiping, slander, untruths, moral values, religious liberty and freedoms, etc.

Martin Luther King Jr. once said "in the end we'll remember not the words of our enemies but the silence of our friends." (2) Howard Cosell, the famous sportscaster once said, "What's right isn't always popular, and what's popular isn't always right." (3)

After World War 2, a German Protestant Pastor, Martin Niemoller stated the matter eloquently when he said, *"First they (the Nazis) came for the Communists, but I didn't speak out because I wasn't a Communist. Then they came for the Socialists, but I didn't speak out because I wasn't a Socialist. Then they came for the trade unionists, but I didn't speak out because I wasn't a trade unionist. Then they came for the Jews, and I didn't speak out because I wasn't a Jew. Then they came for me, but by then there was no one left to speak on my behalf."* (4)

The Utilitarian philosopher, John Stuart Mill famously said, *"All that is necessary for the triumph of evil is that good men remain silent and do nothing."* (5) And we need more brave men and women to choose to stand up and speak out at the right time.

A well-chosen word of wisdom can speak volumes. On the other hand the right word at the wrong time can cause major problems. Mark Twain once said "the right word may be effective, but no word was ever as effective as a rightly timed pause" meaning silence or listening." (6)

An anonymous poet wrote *"A careless word may kindle strife and a cruel word may wreck a life. A bitter word hate instills; a brutal word may smite and kill. But on the other hand a gracious word may smooth the way; a joyous word may light the day. A timely word may* lesson stress; a loving word may heal and bless." (7)

Now to lighten up this teaching a little bit here are a few great thoughts and funny sayings about speaking verses silence or listening.

- An old Greek Proverb says...God gave us teeth to hold back our tongue.

- The great Hebrew poet and philosopher, Solomon Ibn Gabriol has said *"the first step to wisdom is silence; the second step is listening."* (8)

- There are people who instead of listening to what is being said to them are already listening to what they are going to say themselves. (9)

- I don't like people to talk while I'm interrupting. (10)

- Some people would say more if they talk less.

- And someone has prayed this way *"Please Lord, if I can't say something nice today make me keep my big mouth shut.* (11)

- The kindest word in all the world is the unkind word unsaid. (12)

- Well-timed silence hath more eloquence than speech. (13)

- The easiest way to save face is to keep the lower half of it firmly shut. (14)

- Even a fish wouldn't get into trouble if he kept his mouth shut. (15)

- Will Rogers once said *"never miss a good chance to shut-up."* (16)

- I just wish my mouth had a back space key. (17)

- Abraham Lincoln once said *"better to remain silent and be thought a fool than to speak out and remove all doubt."* (18)

- Well-timed silence is the purest speech. (19)

- The great English bard, William Shakespeare, wrote, "*Give every man thine ear, but few thy voice.*" (Pg. 23, "Quick to Listen, Slow to Speak," by Robert Fisher. (20)

- And the last quote is, *"Silence is very valuable; don't break it unless you can improve on it."* (21)

A major problem in our society is that we don't hear enough kind words of wisdom spoken at the right time. As human beings, we crave encouragement and affirmation. I believe God wants our words to be spoken in a timely manner to bring comfort, encouragement, edification and healing that is produced by a pure and positive spirit-controlled mind where we actually speak the words and mind of Christ.

Phil. 2:5 reminds us, *"Let this mind be in you which was also in Christ Jesus."*

Gal. 2:20 states, *"It is no longer I but Jesus who lives in me."*

John 16:13 reads, *"However, when He, the Spirit of truth, has come, He will guide you into all truth; for He will not speak on His own authority, but whatever He hears* He will speak; and He will tell you things to come." Before you speak, ask yourselves these questions; do your words give life? Do they inspire and challenge others to greatness? Who does God want you to encourage through your words today? What would God have to say about what you're saying?

The following scriptures give us greater insight and godly wisdom into having the right motives and timing for speaking appropriate words.

Prov. 12:18 reads, *"Reckless words pierce like a sword, but the tongue of the wise brings healing."*

Prov. 12:25 says, *"An anxious heart weighs a man down, but a kind word cheers him up."*

Prov. 15:23; 26 and 28 declares, *"A man has joy by the answer of his mouth, And a word spoken in due season, how good it is! The thoughts of the wicked are an abomination to the LORD, But the words of the pure are pleasant. The heart of the righteous studies how to answer, But the mouth of the wicked pours forth evil."*

Prov. 16:23-24 reads, *"The heart of the wise teaches his mouth, and adds learning to his lips. Pleasant words are a honeycomb, sweet to the soul and healing to the bones."*

Prov. 31:26 speaking of the virtuous wife, *"She opens her mouth with wisdom, And on her tongue is the law of kindness."*

Isa. 50:4 states, *"The Lord GOD has given Me The tongue of the learned, That I should know how to speak A word in season to him who is weary. He awakens Me morning by morning, He awakens My ear To hear as the learned."* In Prov. 25:11, 12 from the New King James Version, Solomon said, *"A word fitly spoken is like apples of gold in settings of silver. Like an earring of gold and an ornament of fine gold is a wife rebuke to an obedient ear."*

From the Voice Translation of the Bible it reads, *"A well-spoken word at just the right moment is like golden apples in settings of silver. To an attentive ear, constructive criticism from a truly wise person is like an earring or jewelry made of fine gold."*

Knowing the right time to speak is beneficial for both the speaker and hearer, whether they are words of love, encouragement or rebuke.

Col. 4:6 from the Amplified says *"Let your speech at all times be gracious, pleasant and winsome, seasoned as it were with salt, so that you may never be at a loss, to know how you ought to answer anyone who puts a question to you."*

CHAPTER 10

IS IT POSSIBLE TO BRING OUR UNTAMABLE TONGUE UNDER SUBMISSION?

The most difficult of all the spiritual disciplines is bringing your tongue under submission; however it is one of the greatest you can strive for. Why? Because, again your words can either bring forth life or death. James 3:8 says, *"No man can tame the tongue because it is an unruly evil, full of deadly poison."*

On a windswept hill in an English country churchyard stands a drab gray slate tombstone. The faint etching reads "Beneath this stone, a lump of clay, lies Arabella Young, who on the twenty-fourth of May, began to hold her tongue." (1)

If James is correct, there are many who will not gain control over their tongues until they, like Arabella, lie cold in the ground. But there is hope! (2) It is possible to learn how to gain control over your tongues, as we will learn later on in this teaching.

Like us even many of our biblical heroes struggled to control their tongues: (3)

MOSES: Psa. 106:32, 33 says, *"They angered Him also at the waters of strife, So that it went ill with Moses on account of them because they rebelled against His Spirit, So that he spoke rashly with his lips."*

ISAIAH: Isa. 6:5-7 reads, *"So I said: Woe is me, for I am undone! Because I am a man of unclean lips, And I dwell in the midst of a people of unclean lips; For my eyes have seen the King," The LORD of hosts. "Then one of the seraphim flew to me, having in his hand a live coal which he had taken with the tongs from the altar. And he touched my mouth with it, and said: Behold, this has touched your lips; Your iniquity is taken away, And your sin purged."*

JOB: Job 40:4 says, *"Behold, I am vile; what shall I answer You? I lay my hand over my mouth."*

PETER: This disciple of the Lord one day boasted in Mt. 26:33, *"Even if all are made to stumble because of you, I will never be made to stumble."* But that night in Mt. 26:69-75 we find *that Peter sinned with his tongue when he denied knowing Jesus and then cursed and swore saying "I do not know the man."*

Really? "I do not know the man." How that lie must have broken the heart of Jesus! How often do we ourselves break His heart or someone else's? How easy it is to speak hurtful words to and about others.

Throughout the five chapters of James there is something very important to say about the tongue:

In James 1 verses 19, 20, 26 and 27 James admonishes us *"So then, my beloved brethren, let every man be swift to hear, slow to speak, slow to wrath; for the wrath of man does not produce the righteousness of God."*

If anyone among you thinks he is religious, and does not bridle his tongue but deceives his own heart, this one's religion is useless. Pure and undefiled religion before God and the Father is this: to visit orphans and widows in their trouble, and to keep oneself unspotted from the world.

A loose tongue renders our faith absolutely worthless! It can make your every spiritual activity totally useless in God's eyes.

James reference here to "if any among you" means people in the church, in the Body of Christ. Not drug addicts or street people but those members of the body of Jesus who appear pious and spiritual.

They can be anybody, the person who greets visitors at the door, or perhaps even one of the Leaders or Elders in the church. They are active in the work of the Lord, but their tongues are unbridled and out of control! James is zeroing in on those who seem to be holy, kind, gentle and loving, yet who move about the church or their job or their family with acid tongues, always telling tidbits of gossip or listening with a willing ear. They murmur and complain and God says their "religion" all their show of spirituality, is in vain, and worthless! Since many have referred to James' letter as the "Proverbs of the New Testament," we should not be surprised to find much additional information on the use of the tongue in the Old Testament book. (4) Prov. 15:1-4 says, *"A soft answer turns away wrath, But a harsh word stirs up anger. The tongue of the wise uses knowledge rightly, But the mouth of fools pours forth foolishness. The eyes of the LORD are in every place, Keeping watch on the evil and the good. A wholesome tongue is a tree of life, But perverseness in it breaks the spirit."*

I submit to you that the words in verse 3 that says, *"The eyes of the LORD are in every place, Keeping watch on the evil and the good will either give chills of conviction to those who do evil or bring comfort to those who submit to Him."*

Prov. 18:6, 7 declares, *"A fool's lips enter into contention, And his mouth calls for blows. A fool's mouth is his destruction, And his lips are the snare of his soul."*

Prov. 6:16-19 says, *"These six things the LORD hates, Yes, seven are an abomination to Him: A proud look, A lying tongue, Hands that shed innocent blood, A heart that devises wicked plans, Feet that are swift in running to evil, A false witness who speaks lies, And one who sows discord among brethren."* The word "hate" is a very strong word. So is the word abomination which is the Bible's strongest expression of hatred for wickedness. But there are some things that God actually hates, things that are an abomination to Him. Notice he said an ABOMINATION. What I notice is of those seven things, three directly affect the tongues: a lying tongue, a false witness and one who sows discord among the brethren.

Prov. 12:22 declares, *"Lying lips are an abomination to the LORD, But those who deal truthfully are His delight."*

The Bible makes it clear that when you do speak, you are to filter the words that escape your lips. Saints of God need to be reminded! How we need to guard our tongues! How we need to take care that we do not with our tongues produce something that is an abomination to God!

Prov. 13:3 says, *"He who guards his mouth preserves his life, But he who opens wide his lips shall have destruction."*

Prov. 21:23 reads, *"Whoever guards his mouth and tongue keeps his soul from troubles."*

Even though the following three scriptures are not from the book of Proverbs, Peter and Paul also gives us some additional good advice on the use of the tongue from the New Testament.

I Peter 3:10-12 declares, *"For He who would love life And see good days, Let him refrain his tongue from evil, And his lips from speaking deceit. Let him turn away from evil and do good; Let him seek peace and pursue it. For the eyes of the LORD are on the righteous, And His ears are open to their prayers; But the face of the LORD is against those who do evil."*

Now we know when Paul in Romans 3:13-15 lists the five different organs of the body that are the most common vehicles of sin. They are the throat, tongue, lips, mouth and feet. Why? Because four of them relate to speech! (5) And finally, avoid words that reflect poorly on who we are as Christians. In Eph. 4:29-32 the Apostle Paul admonishes, *"Let no corrupt word proceed out of your mouth, but what is good for necessary edification, that it may impart grace to the hearers. And do not grieve the Holy Spirit of God, by whom you were sealed for the day of redemption. Let all bitterness, wrath, anger, clamor, and evil speaking be put away from you, with all malice. And be kind to one another, tenderhearted, forgiving one another, even as God in Christ forgave you."*

Paul's admonition in this scripture sets a strong standard for the righteous use of your words to honor God in each part of your life.

We should and are expected to use words that are pleasing and acceptable to a Holy God.

Curtis Vaughan adds these insightful thoughts about the tongue: *"It can sway men to violence, or it can move them to the noblest actions. It can instruct the ignorant, encourage the dejected, comfort the sorrowing, and soothe the dying. Or it can crush the human spirit, destroy reputations, spread distrust and hate, and bring nations to the brink of war."* (6)

That little two ounce piece of muscle or mucous membrane right under your nose, called the tongue, is the most dangerous and deadliest weapon in the world. It could very well be called a "WMD." A weapon of mass destruction.

The tongue is a badge which you and I wear – it identifies us. It is the greatest index to life. It is the table of contents of our lives. Your speech tells who you are. Your tongue gives you away. It tells where you come from. It tells whether you are ignorant or educated, cultured or crude. Whether you are clean or unclean. Whether you are vulgar or refined. Your tongue tells whether you are a believer or a blasphemer. Whether you are a Christian or a non-Christian and whether you are guilty or not guilty.

If there were a tape recording of every word any person said in a given month, I'm sure that they would not want the world to hear it!

And now we come to James chapter 3, which is all about the tongue. God tests our faith in many ways and one of those ways is by the use of our tongue. James had a fondness of using down-to-earth pictures of the tongue that illustrates meaning. James gives us very wise and important instructions about "The Untamable Tongue" and has a lot to say about its use and abuse. Now this will only be an overview and then I will offer some extra commentary on each of James's illustrations about the tongue.

James 3:1-12 reads from the New King James Version, *"My brethren, let not many of you become teachers, knowing that we shall receive a stricter judgment. For we all stumble in many things. If anyone does not stumble in word, he is a perfect man, able also to bridle the whole body. Indeed, we put bits in horses' mouths that they may obey us, and we turn their whole body. Look also at ships: although they are so large and are driven by fierce winds, they are turned by a very small rudder wherever the pilot desires. Even so the tongue is a little member and boasts great things.*

See how great a forest a little fire kindles! And the tongue is a fire, a world of iniquity. The tongue is so set among our members that it defiles the whole body, and sets on fire the course of nature; and it is set on fire by hell. For every kind of beast and bird, of reptile and creature of the sea, is tamed and has been tamed by mankind. But no man can tame the tongue. It is an unruly evil, full of deadly poison.

With it we bless our God and Father, and with it we curse men, who have been made in the similitude of God. Out of the same mouth proceed blessing and cursing. My brethren, these things ought not to be so. Does a spring send forth fresh water and bitter from the same opening? Can a fig tree, my brethren, bear olives, or a grapevine bear figs? Thus no spring yields both salt water and fresh."

THE BRIDLE AND BIT OF A HORSE

In James, chapter 3 verse 3, James' first illustrations are from two obvious things guided or steered by man in that day, the horse and the ship. He says, *"Indeed, we put bits in horses' mouths that they obey us, and we turn their whole body."*

Without direction a horse can serve no useful purpose to man. It is only when a bit is placed in the horse's mouth that it becomes disciplined and directed. The horse cannot bridle itself; this must be done by man. When the bit is placed in the horse's mouth, the horse can become useful to man's purposes.

A.B. Simpson, Founder of the Christian and Missionary Alliance Church, captures James' argument: *"Just as a man's mouth is the test of his character, so the horse's mouth is the place to control him. We put bits in their mouths, and by these turn about their whole body, so that a little bit of steel and a little thong of leather will hold a fiery steed, (a high-spirited horse), and turn him at the touch of a woman's hand. So the tongue is like a bridle, which can be put upon us. With a fiery horse you put what's known as a curb in his bit. The idea is to hurt him, if he pulls against the bit. So God has given to us checks upon our tongue, making it hurt us, if we speak unadvisedly."* (7)

"In this same way, a person with an unbridled tongue can serve no useful purpose to God. He or she stumbles in many things, especially in the misuse of the mouth. Someone has noted that

almost every sin is in some way related to the abuse of the tongue. So when the tongue is brought under the control of God then man is brought under control as well. The Greek construction in this paragraph goes way beyond the idea of restraining the horse or the man. The concept of bridling describes the process of being led and directed toward a positive goal." (8)

It was King David who said in Psa. 39:1 from the Amplified Bible, *"I said, I will take heed and guard my ways that I may sin not with my tongue. I will muzzle my mouth as with a bridle while the wicked are before me."* In other words David said that because he wanted to give the right kind of testimony he would put a bridle on his mouth.

James 1:26 is worth repeating, *"If anyone among you thinks he is religious, and does not bridle his tongue but deceives his own heart, this one's religion is useless."*

The bridle bits on a horse are not impressive in size, but they can hold a high-spirited horse in check or under control and keeps him from running wild, going in the wrong direction or running in circles. In the same way your tongues can run away and carry you right along with them if they are not bridled. Someone has humorously said of another individual "his mind starts his tongue to wagging and then goes off and leaves it." We as Christians are not to go through life like that. There needs to be a bridle for the tongue.

THE SHIP AND ITS RUDDER

In James 3:4 he uses a second illustration and says, *"Look also at ships: although they are so large and are driven by fierce winds, they are turned by a very small rudder wherever the pilot desires."* (9) This illustration says that large ships can be controlled by a little rudder which few people even see. A fierce storm may drive a ship but a little rudder can control it. What the rudder is to the ship, the tongue is to the human body and the human life. As the rudder controls a ship, so the tongue controls a person.

James 3:5 says that *"the tongue is a little member, and boasts great things."* Amazingly, although the tongue weighs very little, few people are able to hold it. Your tongue can also change the course of your lives for better or worse. Just imagine, people have been ruined by a boneless tongue that's so small and physically so weak. Prov. 15:4 states, *"A deceitful tongue crushes the spirit."*

Obviously a literal fleshly tongue cannot crush the human spirit but the words that are formed by that tongue can. James says that the tongue is more dangerous than a runaway horse or a storm at sea. And it's worth noting that the tongue is condemned more in scripture than alcoholism!

THE FOREST FIRE AND THE SPARK

In the third illustration James compares the tongue to fire. Just as the giant horse is controlled by the tiny bit and the massive ship is governed by the little rudder, so a gigantic fire is started by the tiny spark. The tongue may not be very big, but we do not let its size cause us to underestimate its destructive potential. (10)

He says in James 3:5, 6 from the New Living Translation, *"In the same way, the tongue is a small thing that makes grand speeches. But a tiny spark can set a great forest on fire. And the tongue is a flame of fire. It is a whole world of wickedness, corrupting your entire body. It can set your whole life on fire for it is set on fire by hell itself."* Small spark big fire. That's the way James described the damage done by our reckless and careless words. Fire has been, of course, one of the greatest friends of man and nature. When fire is under control, it warms our bodies, it cooks our food, and it generates power to turn the wheels of industry. But fire is dangerous when it rages out of control. George Washington described it as "the dangerous servant of a fearful master."

Here in Arizona where I live, we are acutely aware of the danger of forest fires. The Rodeo-Chedeski fire of 2002 is the perfect example of the devastation and danger. Two fires were started by a simple strike of a match. They grew, and merged into what was dubbed a "Monster fire" and was one of the worst fires in Arizona history, surpassed only by the Wallow fire of 2011. These dangerous, devastating, absolutely uncontrollable fires had to burn themselves out, in spite of the best efforts of hundreds of firefighters. As we in Arizona are all too aware, brush and forest fires scorch and blacken and are a serious plague.

Today we see great devastations caused by fire. Thousands of people have evacuated their homes and millions of dollars have been spent fighting a blaze that began with a single match. Sadly, we have most recently suffered through the worst devastation and pain caused by wildfires, with the deaths of 19 firefighters known as the "hot shots" in the wildfire of 2013 in the tiny community of Yarnell, Arizona.

Like a fire, the tongue can burn through a church, burn through a community, burn through a town and even burn through a nation. We can see the effects of that in our nation today. The tongue is like fire; when it is under control it's a blessing. When it is out of control it's devastating. The tongue can be a cure or it can be a curse.

The Bible urges us not to underestimate the destructive potential of what we say. One incendiary remark can kindle an inferno of emotional harm. Many times we carelessly toss fiery words about as we pass through life. The best way to avert the flames of anger is to keep from striking that first match. You must let the wisdom of God check your thoughts and hearts before they leave your tongues.

THE ANIMAL AND THE ANIMAL TRAINER

Now we come to the final illustration. James says that we are able to control every kind of beast and animal, but that we have not yet learned how to control the tongue. (11)

James 3:7, 8 reads, *"For every kind of beast and bird, of reptile and creature of the sea, is tamed and has been tamed by mankind. But no man can tame the tongue. It is an unruly evil, full of deadly poison."*

The backdrop of this statement is creation. Gen. 1:26 (paraphrased) tells us, *"Man was to rule over the fish, birds, cattle, and every creeping thing."* When Noah came out of the ark, God reiterated His purpose. Gen. 9:2 says *"And the fear of you and the dread of you shall be on every beast of the earth, on every bird of the air, on all that move on the earth, and on all the fish of the sea. They are given into your hand."* (12)

Today, the nature of the animal has been tamed by the nature of man, (13) due to their innate fear of humans that God instilled in them. We have dancing bears, trained seals, talking dolphins, acrobatic birds, charmed snakes, dogs jumping through hoops, lions with their mouths open wide and the trainer's head inside and elephants marching in line behind one another with riders perched on top.

The instincts of animals can be subdued through conditioning and punishment, but the sinful nature that inspires evil words is beyond our control because the tongue is untamed and untamable without God's help. When man fell into sin, he lost his ability to govern himself. It's interesting to note that Eve in the Garden of Eden was beguiled into sin by the tongue of the serpent through a lie when he said *"you shall not surely die."*

Think about this. The most untamable thing in the world has its den behind your teeth. That's one little thing which no zoo has in captivity, no circus can make it perform. No man can tame it. We can tame a lion; we can tame an elephant, two of the strongest and biggest beasts in all of God's creation but we cannot tame the tongue. Only a regenerate tongue, in a redeemed body, with a tongue tamed by God can be used for Him.

James brings a powerful conclusion to his sermon on the tongue. He cannot conceive of men using the tongue to praise the Lord in one moment and then to destroy each other in the next. In James 3:9, 10 from the New American Standard Bible he says, *"With it we bless our Lord and Father, and with it we curse men, who have been made in the likeness of God; from the same mouth come both blessing and cursing. My brethren, these things ought not to be this way."*

The tongues which you and I have are capable of both praising God and blaspheming Him. When a person can sing like an angel on Sunday and talk like a demon using vile language during the week, the bible calls this person a hypocrite. James 3:11, 12 says, *"Does a spring send forth fresh water and bitter from the same opening? Can a fig tree, my brethren, bear olives, or a grapevine bear figs? Thus no spring yields both salt water and fresh."* In other words, a person can be two-faced, double-minded, and have a forked-tongue...he can say both good and bad. But no fountain on this earth is going to give forth both sweet and bitter water. Nor will a tree bear both figs and olives. I think we can all agree that the tongue can really get us into a lot of trouble. So, what is to be done, then, to tame the tongue?

If God has declared that "no one" can tame the tongue, how can we even begin to bring this destructive force under control? Many people have tried to quit smoking or drinking by the power of the human will. However, the problem of the heart and tongue cannot be solved by that same human will power. It takes the power of the resurrected Christ within us through the Holy Spirit to control the tongue...and that power is available only to those who turn their lives over to Him.

Romans 8:10-17 declares, *"And if Christ is in you, the body is dead because of sin, but the Spirit is life because of righteousness. But if the Spirit of Him who raised Jesus from the dead dwells in you, He who raised Christ from the dead will also give life to your mortal bodies through His Spirit who dwells in you. Therefore, brethren, we are debtors—not to the flesh, to live according to the flesh. For if you live according to the flesh you will die; but if by the Spirit you put to death the deeds of the body, you will live. For as many as are led by the Spirit of God, these are sons of God. For you did not receive the spirit of bondage again to fear, but you received the Spirit of adoption by whom we cry out, 'Abba, Father.' The Spirit Himself bears witness with our spirit that we are children of God, and if children, then heirs—heirs of God and joint heirs with Christ, if indeed we suffer with Him, that we may also be glorified together."*

And as with so many things in life, according to Jesus in Mt. 19:26, *"With men this is impossible but with God all things are possible."* There is only one who can control or tame the tongue. Only by God's Holy Spirit living within us can we hope to gain control over our tongues. But something is required on your part. You have to want to let God have that control.

He convicts you when you sin with your lips and that conviction drives you to repent and pray for more of His Holy Spirit in your lives to influence you and give you power so you can avoid further sin. As you cling to Him and yield to Him in obedience He controls you more and more including your tongues. God is saying something very important here and that can be life changing if you will receive it and act upon it.

In the Old Testament, God spoke about the transforming power that would be available to His people through a new covenant He would make with them.

Speaking about this new covenant Jer. 31:31-34 declares, *"Behold, the days are coming, says the LORD, when I will make a new covenant with the house of Israel and with the house of Judah— not according to the covenant that I made with their fathers in the day that I took them by the hand to lead them out of the land of Egypt, My covenant which they broke, though I was a husband to them, says the LORD. But this is the covenant that I will make with the house of Israel after those days, says the LORD: I will put My law in their minds, and write it on their hearts; and I will be their God, and they shall be My people. No more shall every man teach his neighbor, and every man his brother, saying, 'Know the LORD,' for they all shall know Me, from the least of them to the greatest of them, says the LORD. For I will forgive their iniquity, and their sin I will remember no more."*

Then in Ezek. 36:26-28 God said, *"I will give you a new heart and put a new spirit within you; I will take the heart of stone out of your flesh and give you a heart of flesh. I will put my spirit within you and cause you to walk in my statutes, and you will keep my judgments to do them. Then you shall dwell in the land that I gave to your father, you shall be my people, and I will be your God."*

In closing I want you to realize that this New Covenant and new spirit was poured out to you at Pentecost and continues to flow today. According to the book of Hebrews through His sacrificial death for sin once and for all time, Jesus, the mediator of this New Covenant has made it possible for all believers, Jew and Gentile, to receive the spirit's divine enabling power to be over-comers of any sin in our lives including power to control the words we speak. And again this is available to all who place their faith in the resurrected Yeshua Ha-Mashiach, Jesus the Messiah.

Let me leave you with these final thoughts. One day your voice will be silent after breathing your last breath so make the most out of the words you speak while you still have breath using Godly wisdom in all you say for His honor and glory.

END NOTES

Chapter 1

1. Fisher, Robert E. *"Quick to Listen, Slow to Speak,"* pg 9, 1960, Pathway Press, Cleveland TN, Republished 1987
2. Sedler, Dr. Michael D, *"When to Speak Up and When to Shut Up."* pg. 16, 2003, Chosen Books, a division of Baker Publishing Group
3. *Ibid*, pg. 137
4. *Ibid*, pg 16
5. *Ibid*

Chapter 2

1. Jaynes, Sharon, *"The Power of a Woman's Words,"* pgs 19-20, 2007, Harvest House Publishers,

Chapter 3

1. Dickenson, Emily *"The Complete Poems, 1850 – 1870."* Edited by Thomas H. Johnson, Bay Back Books, 1976.
2. TheFreshmanSurvivalGuide.com, *"When it's online, it's there forever."* Chapter 15.

Chapter 4

1. Huffpost Healthy Living, *"Be careful of your thoughts, for your thoughts become your words. Be careful of your words, for your words become your actions. Be careful of your actions, for your actions become your habits. Be careful of your habits, for*

your habits become your character. Be careful of your character, for your character becomes your destiny." Chinese Proverb, Author Unknown. TheHuffingtonPost.com, 4/28/2014
  2. Rowling, J K, *Harry Potter and the Order of the Phoenix,* Scholastic, Inc 2004

Chapter 5
  1. Christ, Jesus. Paraphrase of the bible verse Matthew 12:34, *"For out of the overflow of the heart, the mouth speaks."*

Chapter 6
  1. Jaynes, Sharon, "The Power of a Woman's Words,"pg 25, 2007 Harvest House Publishers,
  2. *Ibid,* pg 13
  3. Ibid, pg. 13-18: (original story by Ballard, Elizabeth Silance, *"Three Letters From Teddy,"* Home Life Magazine, 1974)
  4. *Ibid,* pg 25 - 29
  5. Irving, Washington, *"Rip Van Winkle,"* The Sketch Book of Geoffrey Crayon, 1819
  6. 2013 Elda Just, "The Power of Encouragement," email endorsement by Cindy Jacobs.
  7. Nelson, Thomas, "New King James Study Bible, 2nd Edition" Thomas Nelson Publisher 2013

Chapter 8
  1. Inrig, Gary, *"Quality Friendship, The Risks and Rewards,"* pg 52-53, Moody Publishers 1988

Chapter 9
  1. Anonymous, English nursery rhyme, original version published in *Punch*, April 10, 1875. Original version reads, *"There was an owl liv'd in*

an oak, The more he heard, the less he spoke, The less he spoke, the more he heard. O, if men were all like that wise bird."

2. King, Jr., Martin Luther, *"The Trumpet of Conscience,"* speech from Steeler Lecture, November 1967.
3. Cosell, Howard, *"Like It Is,"* Playboy Press, 1974.
4. Niemoller, Martin, *"The Confessing Church,"* speech given in Frankfurt, Germany, January 6, 1946.
5. Mill, John Stuart, *"Inaugural Address at the University of St. Andrew,"* Fife, Scotland, United Kingdom, February 1, 1867
6. Twain, Mark, *"The Complete Speeches of Mark Twain,"* e-book, e-artnow publishers, 2014
7. Unknown, as printed in *"30 Days to Taming your Tongue: What you say (and don't say) will improve your relationships"* by Deborah Smith Pegues. Harvest House Publishers April 2005
8. Ibn Gabirol, Solomon, *"The first step in the acquisition of wisdom is silence, the second listening, the third memory, the fourth practice, the fifth teaching others."* Hebrew poet and philospher, b. 1021, d.1058
9. Guinon, Albert, French Playwright, b. 1863, d. 1923.
10. Nour, David, Actual Quote "I'll excuse you for talking while I'm interrupting," *Relationship Economics: Transform Your Most Valuable Busines Contacts Into Personal and Professional Success."* Wiley publishers, 2011.
11. Black, Rick, *"Tiny Loan Association Is A Page From Yesteryear,"* Chicago Tribune, March 18, 1994.
12. Unknown, Quoted in *"Delicious,"* 808delicious.blogspot.com, January 6, 2012.

13. Tupper, Martin Farquhar, *"Proverbial Philosophy,"* Forgotten Books publisher, 2012, originally published in 1837.
14. Quote attributed to "Ann Landers." (Lederer, Esther Pauline b. 1918, d. 2002)
15. Old Korean Proverb.
16. Quote attributed to Will Rogers, b. 1879, d. 1935
17. Unknown Author.
18. Quote attributed to Lincoln, Abraham b. 1812, d. 1865
19. Tupper, Martin Farquhar, *"Ibid."*
20. Fisher, Robert *"Quick to Listen, Slow to Speak,"* pg. 23, 1960, Pathway Press, Cleveland TN, Republished 1987
21. Vander Heyden, Carol, *"A Touch of Class,"* Trafford Publishing, 2003

Chapter 10
1. Jeremiah, David, Dr. *"What To Do When You Don't Know What To Do,"* Chapter 6, pgs 245-246, Victor Books/SP Publications, 1993
2. *Ibid*
3. *Ibid*
4. *Ibid*
5. *Ibid*
6. *Ibid*
7. *Ibid*
8. *Ibid*
9. *Ibid*
10. *Ibid,* pg 106
11. *Ibid,* pg 108
12. *Ibid,* pg 108
13. *Ibid,* pg 108

ABOUT THE AUTHOR

Pastor and Messianic Rabbi Gil Kaplan is one of the pioneers in the Messianic Jewish movement.

This author and passionate teacher is an anointed expositor of God's Word who has been appointed by the Lord to stand in the office of pastor and teacher. His profound, systematic, revelatory teachings have blessed a diverse audience of believers.

His father, Evangelist Louis Kaplan, founded *Jewish Voice Ministries International* in 1967. Not only does Pastor Gil hold a Master's Degree in Theology, he is a licensed Messianic Rabbi under the covering of Rabbi Jonathan Bernis, the current President and CEO of JVMI.

Pastor Gil has served as Pastor/Rabbi for several Messianic Congregations/Fellowships, frequently teaching at various Bible Colleges and is a popular seminar and conference speaker.

Gil and his wife, Pastor Brenda Kaplan are Co-founders of *Builders of Unity Ministries International* in Phoenix, Arizona. They are both ordained Pastors through Church for the Nations in Phoenix, Arizona under the pastoral covering of Dr. Michael and Mary Maiden, where they also faithfully attend services. The Kaplans reside in Glendale, Arizona.

Some of Pastor Gil Kaplan's most popular teachings are:

1. The Power of Spoken and Unspoken Words
2. Our Tears are Precious
3. In Brokenness there is Strength
4. Our Time is Precious.....Use it Wisely (series)

The Jewish Roots of the Christian Faith such as:

1. The history of Israel
2. World-wide Anti-Semitism
3. The Miracle of Israel's Preservation
4. Israel's many symbols: Shofar/Ram's Horn, Mezuzah, Prayer Shawl, Tefillin/Phylacteries
5. Israel's many Feasts and Festivals that all point to Yeshua/Jesus as their fulfillment.

BUILDERS OF UNITY MINISTRIES INTERNATIONAL

Website: www.buildersofunity.org

Email: kaplanbk2003@yahoo.com

Telephone: 623-444-6146